The Art of Preserving Flowers

A guide for Canadians

The Art of Preserving Flowers

Elizabeth MacDermot

James Lewis & Samuel, Publishers
Toronto
1973

ISBN 0-88862-041-1 cloth
ISBN 0-88862-042-X paper

Printed and bound in Canada

Designed by Lynn Campbell
4 3 2 1 73 74 75 76

James Lewis and Samuel, Publishers
Egerton Ryerson Memorial Building
35 Britain Street
Toronto 299, Canada

Table of Contents

In memory of Ruth Foster Haldenby

"The greatest art that the world has ever produced is the art of beautifying and making home attractive . . . . the grandest and noblest motives that can stir the human heart are those awakened within the pale of domestic life. Beautiful art can only be inspired by pure and beautiful thoughts, and unless some elements of taste and beauty are provided for the leisure hours at home, how can it be expected that the young may find their homes more attractive than places of sin and amusement, and have pure thoughts, pure hearts and a love of refinement."

from The Popular Art Instructor,
published by J. B. Young & Co.,
Windsor and Toronto, 1887.

Acknowledgments

The preservation of flowers in their original shapes and colours is a specialty of a group of people associated with my shop, Flower and Green Decorations of Montreal. It is an art practiced chiefly by individuals and members of garden clubs. Seldom has it been carried on by a commercial florist. Though a considerable amount has been published on the subject, our experience has taught us a host of labour-saving techniques which have never appeared in print.

I am greatly indebted to a number of people who have been involved with this book; Dorothy Kimpton, whom I first met at Christ Church Cathedral at Thanksgiving time nearly a quarter of a century ago, and to whom I have been giving thanks ever since; also, Denny Morgan and his wife, Pat, who have contributed so much from their farm near Lancaster, Ontario, to this book.

Anne Boake and her husband, Roy, have made their city garden bloom for us, as has Betty Piper, with her beautiful garden overlooking the Lake of Two Mountains. Ancilla Deghenghi has brought not only her garden flowers to our shop but also her knowledge and love of flowers from her native Italy. Practically all the flowers you see in the photographs came from these four gardens.

We are greatly honoured to have the excellent chapter on wildflowers and ferns from Dorothy Swales, Ph.D., Honorary Curator of McGill University Herbarium, and recently retired Curator of Macdonald College Herbarium.

I also appreciate the amount of time and interest Douglas Dawson has given to photography of the procedure and the arrangements, as did S. Posen, who also contributed photographs. There are many others to thank, but in particular, Isabel Pohlmann, Eleanor Luke, Molly Pettit, Heather Holt, and Patricia Wood, who gave so willingly of their special skills; and Ron Armstrong, who photographed Pat Morgan's gardens and the bounty of her harvest. And last but not the least by far, my greatest supporter, my husband, Pembroke Noel MacDermot.

Dandelions, edelweiss, exacum, and harebells preserved in silica gel and arranged in a miniature triangular mass design.

Introduction

In 1956 three women decided to go into business together preparing flowers for weddings and parties, and with a little courage and less capital, a lawyer, and an accountant, so was born Flower and Green Decorations, Registered. The name was partly cribbed from the English flower decorator, the late Constance Spry, who had called her first business, "Flower Decorations". It was in 1968 that I moved from an upstairs office to a shop and became an honest to God shopkeeper.

I received my professional training from my former partner, Irene Davies, who trained at an excellent school for commercial florists in Chicago. She was a perfectionist. But my early training, which perhaps influenced me most, was at my mother's knee. My mother never walked down a country lane without bringing home a bunch of wildflowers, grasses and ferns. I used to marvel how she could make such simple flowers look so beautiful in a vase. My father was the gardener. From both of them, as well as from the land of my childhood, I inherited a love of flowers.

Southwestern Ontario is called the garden of Ontario. Its rich farmland supplies fruits and vegetables for the large canneries in that part of the country. In my day it was not only fruits and vegetables that grew in profusion, for we all had gardens full of flowers, and a few town houses also had conservatories. My grandfather's house had a small conservatory which I dearly loved in the wintertime, and there was a greenhouse nearby which I haunted from the time I could walk. I remember well the look on the face of the busy florist when Little Bessie appeared with her endless questions. But nothing could keep me from exploring the fascinating flowers that grew under the benches, and the bright green moss that clung to the rotting wood. I saw that same helpless look on faces in other florist's shops and greenhouses, those places which I have always found irresistible over the years.

What a delight it was to eat fresh green peas right out of the pods, and sun-warmed tomatoes and strawberries. I suppose there were better gardens in Canada, but to me those at Highbanks on Lake Erie were the best. But that was many years ago, when summers were pure enchantment and Highbanks had a mystique of its own, especially when Monarch butterflies congregated there by the thousands on their migration to the South. I visited Highbanks recently, and found the climbing roses that my father had planted along the orchard fence more than fifty years ago were a mass of glorious pink bloom; but many of the old gardens had gone over the banks into the lake because of erosion along the shoreline. But the memories were still there, tangled with flowers: the childhood games of charades, acting out words like snap-dragon, foxglove, and Canterbury bells.

It is old-fashioned today to speak of love affairs, but this is what we have with flowers. But there is one difference; while the old *affair de coeur* too often quickly passed, ours, starting with the first bunch of dandelions we clutched in our small, chubby hands at the age of two, has continued throughout the years. And, as that first clutch of dandelions was presented to our nearest and dearest, so we give you our ''dandelions'', preserved with love for your winter bouquets.

Chapter 1 Dried and Preserved Flowers: The Difference

As modern medicine can now prolong the life of man, so modern techniques can achieve almost the same thing for flowers. The blossoms of spring and summer can be preserved in colour and shape so perfectly that at first glance the eye can make us believe that we are looking at a bowl of freshly picked flowers. The disbeliever has to touch to be convinced, which can be disastrous to the fragile bloom.

We make a distinction between drying and preserving flowers. Dried flowers and plants dry naturally by hanging and/or by standing upright in an airy, dark, dry place. The category includes some wildflowers, weeds, grasses, and some cultivated flowering plants which are in the so-called everlasting class; as well as a few that are not, such as delphiniums. This method is old and well-known, and we will discuss it in some detail in Chapter Seven.

There are other ways that plant material can be dried, by pressing, as we do ferns, or by treatment with glycerine, which is most successful for certain branches and seed heads. These also will be dealt with in Chapter Seven.

The preservation of flowers, though it too has an ancient history, never reached a peak of perfection until quite recently. To preserve flowers, they must be buried completely in a drying agent. Various kinds of dessicating materials have been used, but for general purposes, silica gel has proved by far the most useful. This book deals chiefly with silica gel treatment, and the method will be described fully, step by step.

Through our experience in a flower shop, where preserved flower arrangements are made up by the hundreds during the fall and winter, we have developed a simple technique that makes the older methods seem complicated and labourious. There is no doubt that the process is still time-consuming, but through growing fascination with it, you can soon be lost to the world, some of which we could happily lose!

Top: Flowers being air-dried.
Bottom: Flowers being prepared for preservation in silica gel.

5

This copper vase contains a natural arrangement of Woburn Abbey, Tropicana, and Forever Yours roses, preserved in silica gel.

Chapter 2   Preserving Flowers: The Reasons Why

Why this craze for preserved flowers? Flower growers, commercial and amateur, listen with horror while we enthusiastically tell them of our success in treating flowers with silica gel.

A few years ago, when we were in dire need of garden flowers, a friend who has a lovely garden called me to say that I could take what I wanted from her garden for drying, since she herself had not the slightest interest in it. I gladly accepted her invitation and as we were cutting, she mused, "Perhaps I should try to dry a few of the Tropicana roses. They are my husband's favourites." And she did preserve them, with great success. The next summer she organized a group to preserve her flowers, to press ferns, and to collect grasses and seed pods. We bought all of them for the shop, and since that time, her interest and enthusiasm has helped tremendously to further the growth and the scope of our work.

It does take time to interest the ardent gardener. He cannot bear the thought of burying his lovely blossoms at the peak of their bloom in a bluish-white sand. But what pleasure it gives him during the winter to see his roses still "blooming" on his mantlepiece!

Though dried flowers and sweet-smelling herbs have been used to decorate homes through the centuries, they have reached a popularity today quite unknown before. Many varieties of everlasting flowers can be grown here in Canada, and our fields and woods, mountains and seashores produce endless materials that can be collected and dried. A great deal that one sees on the market is imported. Some, of course, cannot be cultivated in Canada; hand-made flowers made from seeds of flowers, fruits, and vegetables come chiefly from Italy and Mexico.

There is hardly a flower shop today that does not carry a large range of dried flowers in addition to fresh ones, and many food stores, department stores, and gift shops sell them. Most of them are dyed to match the latest fashions in home decorating.

Few shops carry preserved flowers. They are not practical because they are very fragile and need careful handling. Climate, also, makes a difference to their lasting quality. They can wilt in high humidity and therefore should only be used during the months when houses are heated.

One reason for substituting dried flowers for fresh ones is the high cost of flowers. With the exception of the southwest coast, the growing season in Canada is short, and labour and transportation costs are high. More and more big commercial growers are cutting back on the varieties they stock, saying that they are not covering their costs. It is true that the price of flowers has not risen in proportion to increases in other fields, but to the consumer the price of flowers makes them a luxury item.

To achieve variety, Canadian florists have to depend on foreign growers. Large shipments come into the Montreal area, for instance, from the United States daily and from Europe at least once a week. The cost of transportation is a major factor in the price of these flowers. It is the greatest pity that flowers have become a luxury, because their appeal is universal.

But there are other reasons for preserving flowers. In dry, heated homes or apartments it is difficult for even the freshest flowers to last long. Greenhouse plants, used to a high degree of humidity, have to struggle to survive, and their owner struggles along with them. Also, most people lead busy lives; gone are the days when the lady of the house spent her mornings doing the flowers. You are expected to arrange your flowers, and that takes time, much more time and equipment than the old method of just popping them into a vase, blissfully ignorant of rules laid down by people who are dictators in such matters. And then, after all your trouble, they must eventually wither and die.

But mankind must have flowers. From earliest times they have played an important part in history. They have been cherished for their religious and symbolic significance, praised in song and verse, painted by the world's greatest artists, carved in stone and wood, and incorporated into the finest tapestries and illuminated parchments. They have been used in many ways for many reasons, but not until comparatively recent times were they arranged in vases to decorate the home.

Flower arranging, as we think of it today, is a twentieth-century phenomenon. It is fascinating to note the important role that flowers have played in the past and still do play in all decorative arts, revealing man's need to be surrounded by flowers. We have only to glance through the pages of any magazine that specializes in interior decorating to see that they accent every nook and cranny of the house.

I must not be too critical of artificial flowers; there are some very good ones, but there are others that hurt the eye as a high, piercing sound can hurt the ear. It is so much better to have the real thing if we can. Wild plants and flowers grow everywhere, even within our great, grimy cities, in vacant lots, and along railroad tracks, canals and rivers. To some people they are just weeds, but they can make attractive bouquets, either fresh or dried. If you long for colour, a few drops of vegetable dye will do the trick. Many of the colourful dried flowers that are sold in the shops are just the same weeds, grasses or grains which are free for the taking. Even in winter you can find lovely brown dried weeds, grasses, and seed pods showing above the snow. Once you start looking, a whole new world opens up to you.

People who are lucky enough to have been brought up in the country, or at least to have spent vacations out of the city, are apt to forget the many thousands of city-dwellers whose landscape consists only of pavement and the row of houses across the street. These people simply do not see growing, living plants. They never know the joys that they are missing.

One day when I was riding down Sherbrooke Street in Montreal in a taxicab, I caught sight of a ginkgo tree in all its shimmering, rich yellow autumn finery. It was so startlingly beautiful that I cried out, "Look at that tree!"

The driver slammed on his brakes, turned and said, "Lady, what did you say?"

"Look at that tree," I said. "It's so beautiful!"

The driver did not say anything for a few minutes as he continued along the road, but finally he mused, "You know, I've never seen a tree before. I guess I just never thought about them."

Chapter 3   The History of Flower-Preserving
by Patricia Morgan, O.D.H.

Studying the history of preserved plants is particularly difficult because all of the evidence, that is, the plant material itself, has long since disappeared. The dust of ages covers leaves and petals that may once have graced the caves of the Neanderthal Man. However, there are cave drawings that show that flowers were objects of wonder, if not of love, even in Neolithic times. In the *Bible*, Matthew 23 mentions paying the "tithe of mint and anise and cummin", which plants were dried for future use. Preserved lotus petals and seeds were found in the tomb of Tutankhamen. A fresco in the Egyptian tomb of Nebamun and Ipuky (1380 B.C.) shows bulrushes and papyrus arranged in patterns that celebrated the frozen formality of death. These first allusions tell us that mankind has long been attempting to preserve the fragile beauty and utilitarian properties of plants.

An Egyptian limestone wall relief sculpture from the nineteenth dynasty, Ramses. The three offerers, Queen Tuya with two members of the nobility, cary vases of lotus flowers. Such scenes occur frequently in Egyptian tombs, where flowers were often placed on top of the mummy itself, and have been found perfectly preserved in recent times. Courtesy of the Royal Ontario Museum, Toronto.

Millemorbia & Caſtrangula dicitur. Germanicè **Krau-nvvurtz, Sauvvurtz, groſz feiguuartz en kraut.** [Galli-
Galeopſis. cè *l'Herbe aux chats.*] Appoſitè autem Galeopſis appellatur, nomine ex Græco & Latino compoſito , quòd eius flores prorſus galeæ aſpectum referant. Aut ſi Græca cũ Latinis componi haud poſſunt. γαλκοψις cum μ & non ι, vt habent multa exemplaria, ſcribendum erit, vt idem valeat ac Mu-ſtelæ aſpectum referens: flores enim non diſſimiles eſſe ca-piti illius animalis videntur. Et ita legédũ eſſe Plinius etiã teſtatur, qui Galeopſin hanc nominat herbam. Scrophu-lariam autem à curandis ſtrumis, quas ſcrophulas vocant, recentiores, dixerunt.

FORMA.

Totus cum ſuo caule & foliis frutex Vrticæ ſimilis eſt, læuiora tamé habet folia & cum terũ-tur grauiter odorata . Flores illi tenues, & pur-puraſcentes . Huius de-lineationis notæ in vni-uerſum omnes, nulla prſ-ſus reclamante , herbæ quam vulgus Scrophu-lariam maiorem nomi-nat, conueniunt . Frutex enim eſt qui ad humani corporis ferè longitudi-nem interdum aſſurgit, foliaque Vrticæ habet, ſed læuiora, & quæ trita grauem fundunt odoré, Flores tenues, atque pur puraſcentes . Reſpondet etiã locus natalis, vt ex ſequentibus patebit. Eſſe autem veterum Galeo-pſin

Galeopſis ſiue Scrophula-ria maior.

A Chinese ancestor portrait from the Ch'ing Dynasty, nineteenth century, perhaps executed for a birthday, of a Mongol military official and his wife in full court dress. Deer, crane, pine, bamboo, peaches and chrysanthemums are all symbols of longevity. Flower gardens played an impor-tant part in the culture of the Chinese, and the arrangement included in the portrait indicates the auspicious qualities of the ancestors. Courtesy of the Royal Ontario Museum, Toronto.

Two pages from *Des Historia Stirpium*, an early herbal pub-lished in 1549 and written by Leonharto Fuchs. The format shown on these pages was followed for each separate herb, and was used in herbals for centuries to come. It provides

pſin vulgi Scrophulariam maiorem,præter ea que iam di-
ximus,manuſcriptus quoque codex euidenter oſtendit:in
quo pictura ita Scrophulariam refert,vt nemo ſit qui eam
non agnoſcat.Huc accedit quòd in deſcriptione,quam ex
Dioſcoride deſumpſit,apertè teſtatur Scrophulariam maiorem alio nomine dictam eſſe Galeopſin & Galeobdolõ.
Neq; facultates diſcrepât,ſed vtrarûque ſimiles ſunt,adeò
vt haud dubiè veterum Galeopſis,recentiorum herbario-
rum ſit Scrophularia maior.

LOCVS.

Naſcitur circa ſepes,ſemitasque , & in areis ædificiorũ
paſsim.

TEMPVS.

Colligitur Iunio & Iulio mẽſibus,tum enim potiſsimũ
floret.

TEMPERAMENTVM.

Deſiccat,extenuat,& diſcutit,adeòque partium eſt te-
nuiũ, id qd amaritudo quã in guſtu prę ſe fert,ſatis idicat.

VIRES EX DIOSCORIDE.

Folia,ſuccus,caulis & ſemen,duritias,carcinomata,ſtru
mas,parotidas & panos deijciunt.Oportet autem bis die
cum aceto tepidum cataplaſma imponere.Fouentur & decocto eius vtiliter.Ad nomas,gangrænas,& putreſcentia
cum ſale illita proſunt.

EX PAVLO.

Galeopſis,quam alii Galeobdolon appellant,vrticæ ſimilis herba eſt,maiorem tamen lęuorem habet,& odorem
grauem,Scirrhoſos tumores diſsipat & emollit.Itẽ ad nomas cataplaſmatis modo illita confert.

EX PLINIO.

Galeopſis folia caulesq;,duritias & carcinomata ſanât
ex aceto trita & impoſita.Itẽ ſtrumas,panos & parotidas
diſcutiunt.Ex vſu eſt & decocto ſucco fouere.Putreſcẽtia
quoque & gangrænas ſanat.

APPENDIX.

Recentiores etiam Scrophulariæ tribuunt facultatẽ ſa-
nandi vlcera putreſcẽtia,& mariſcas.Succum eius mederi

n ii	de-

a detailed physical description, a note on habitat and season
of bloom, and lenghty description of the medicinal properties
of the herbs, which were air-dried for year-round use. Courtesy of the University of Toronto Rare Books Library.

The Japanese have a long history of flower arranging, and
the Chinese learned to preserve plant materials centuries ago.
But the first European to write about plants was the Greek
Theophrastus, called the Father of Botany, who was born
in 370 B.C. He was a pupil of Plato and later of Aristotle.
Writing about everyday life at the height of the Greek Empire,
he mentions wreath and garland-flower makers, presumably
the ''florists'' of their day, and adds that their favourites
were gilliflowers and wallflowers. Pliny, born 23 A.D., also
mentions that parsley wreaths were made for victors in the
sacred contests of the Nemean Games, as well as laurel foliage
wreaths, which crowned the victors in the Pythian Games
and designated certain offices and functions.

Books known as herbals were a continuing compilation
of herb lore. They were a mixture of medicinal remedies,
cooking recipes, and botanical descriptions of plants, and
were a household encyclopedia for those who could read
in the medieval monasteries and castles. They advocated the
use of all kinds of dried plant materials for medicine, flavouring and essence.

By Elizabeth I's reign, household gardens were common,
and flowers from these beautifully designed gardens were
used in homes for decoration and also for enhancing milady's
costume, as we can see today in many famous paintings.
Great quantities of aromatic herbs were grown and dried
not only for medicinal and savoury use, but also for strewing
on the floors of churches and banquet halls as well as for
the dining table. As sanitary precautions were non-existent,
the sweet-smelling herbs helped to freshen the air. It was
also believed that some of the herbs had antiseptic qualities.
Little bags of dried herbs and sweet-smelling flower petals
were sometimes worn around the neck as an amulet to ward
off evil spirits.

In 1638, P. Giovanni Battista Ferrari of Siena published
the first written account of the then-popular art of drying
flowers in sand, in his book *Flora —ouero Cultura di Fiori*.

But while the educated and wealthy were reading the works
of an ancient Greek or Roman to learn about herbs, the less
fortunate people were out gathering flowers, seeds, roots,
leaves, and bark, and were learning by trial-and-error the
properties of herbs for healing or poisoning, and also for
flavouring and scenting. Many a woman who was an excellent
herbalist was burned at the stake for being a witch.

The North American Indians were using preserved plants
to heal their sick and to make dyes and poisons long before
Europeans arrived, but when the settlers came, they brought
with them seeds and roots of plants from Europe.

The joy of drying flowers and arranging them to enhance

the interiors of homes evolved naturally from the hanging and drying of herbs in the house. Early garden books tell us that dried flowers were used to decorate the home in the winter season. Flowers for drying were commonly called "everlasting", and they included the pearly everlasting, globe amaranth and strawflowers. Phillip Miller (1691-1771), when writing of them in his *Figures of Plants*, says that these flowers "were brought to the Markets in great plenty during the winter season, to adorn rooms. The Gardeners had a Method of staining them a deep red and blue colour, by dipping them into different liquids, so they brought them to the Markets in bunches of four different colours; white, purple, blue and red: and when their stalks were put into glasses with sand, the flowers would continue in beauty till the Spring". Miller also edited *The Gardener's Dictionary*; he wrote of the globe amaranth: "The flowers, if gathered before they decay on the plant, and kept in a dry place, will remain in beauty for some years, especially if they are not too much expos'd to the air". He added that when mixed with other varieties of plants, they "make a curious variety of dry flowers for basons to adorn rooms in the winter season, when few other kinds are to be had". Peter Collinson, who is believed to have introduced more than forty American plants into English gardens, also mentions the amaranth, saying that, "if the flowers are gathered in perfection and hung up with their heads downwards in a dry shady room, they will keep their colours for years and will make a pleasant ornament to adorn the windows of your parlor or study all the winter".

Peter Kalm (1715-1779), writes in his *Travels into North America* of colonists gathering pearly everlastings in great quantities for winter decoration, calling them "life everlasting" because of their changelessness, fresh or dried.

Gardening for the average Canadian gradually went beyond the necessity of raising vegetables and herbs for personal use; it became a hobby as well, and flowers for beauty and decoration were added. Our ancestors exchanged roots, slips, plants and seeds in order to have variety in their gardens as well as to sample something "new" from the seed catalogues. They carefully stored the tender plants over winter, filling their window sills with greenery. Our first settlers would not have bothered with house plants, due to the lack of light indoors and the extremes of temperature.

A selection from *The Complete Herbal* by Nicholas Culpeper, originally published in 1653. This became the most popular herbal in English, and was used throughout North America and England through the nineteenth century. This passage is from an 1835 edition. Courtesy of the Metropolitan Toronto Library.

DANDELION, VULGARLY CALLED PISS-A-BEDS.

Descript.] It is well known to have many long and deep gashed leaves, lying on the ground round about the head of the roots; the ends of each gash or jag, on both sides looking downwards towards the roots; the middle rib being white, which being broken, yields abundance of bitter milk, but the root much more; from among the leaves, which always abide green, arise many slender, weak, naked foot-stalks, every one of them bearing at the top one large yellow flower, consisting of many rows of yellow leaves, broad at the points, and nicked in with deep spots of yellow in the middle, which growing ripe, the green husk wherein the flowers stood turns itself down to the stalk, and the head of down becomes as round as a ball: with long seed underneath, bearing a part of the down on the head of every one, which together is blown away with the wind, or may be at once blown away with one's mouth. The root growing downwards exceedingly deep, which being broken off within the ground, will yet shoot forth again, and will hardly be destroyed where it hath once taken deep root in the ground.

Place.] It grows frequently in all meadows and pasture-grounds.

Time.] It flowers in one place or other almost all the year long.

Government and virtues.] It is under the dominion of Jupiter. It is of an opening and cleansing quality, and therefore very effectual for the obstructions of the liver gall and spleen, and the diseases that arise from them, as the jaundice and hypocondriac; it opens the passages of the urine both in young and old; powerfully cleanses imposthumes and inward ulcers in the urinary passage, and by its drying and temperate quality doth afterwards heal them; for which purpose the decoction of the roots or leaves in white wine, or the leaves chopped as pot-herbs, with a few Alisanders, and boiled in their broth, are very effectual. And whoever is drawing towards a consumption or an evil disposition of the whole body, called Cachexia, by the use hereof for some time together, shall find a wonderful help. It helps also to procure rest and sleep to bodies distempered by the heat of ague fits, or otherwise: The distilled water is effectual to drink in pestilential fevers, and to wash the sores.

You see here what virtues this common herb hath, and that is the reason the French and Dutch so often eat them in the Spring; and now if you look a little farther, you may see plainly without a pair of spectacles, that foreign physicians are not so selfish as ours are, but more communicative of the virtues of plants to people.

Early Canadian settlers hung herbs to dry in a warm, dry place in their first homes. These were the only indoor plants in Canada in the early dwellings. Photo taken at Black Creek Pioneer Village, courtesy of The Metropolitan Toronto and Region Conservation Authority.

This elegant arrangement of waxed flowers under a bell jar rests on a mantlepiece at Dundern Castle, Hamilton, Ontario. From *At Home in Upper Canada* by Jeanne Minhinnick, published by Clarke, Irwin and Company Limited.

As the settlements prospered and afforded their residents more leisure time, dried-flower craft became more and more popular. This mat made of pressed wildflowers was made in rural Ontario in the early 1800's. Courtesy of the Royal Ontario Museum, Toronto. Gift of Mr. G. Alex Forbes.

13

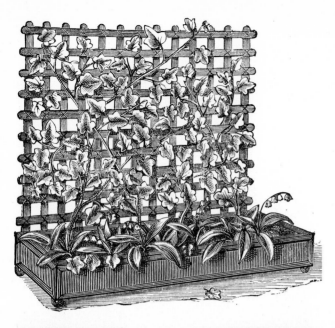

The Victorians loved to preserve flowers from the funerals of their dear departed, and they liked to camouflage all sorts of things with flowers preserved through laborious and time-consuming methods. These three examples are taken from *The Popular Art Instructor*, published by J. B. Young and Company in Windsor, Ontario, in 1887.

Instead they had dried branches of leaves, berries or seed pods placed in a jug, and aromatic herbs hung from the rafters. Toward the middle of the nineteenth century, Canadians were prospering and were able to leave the original cabin for a finer home. Some of the dawn-to-dark bondage of hard work was behind them, and the women had time for enhancing their homes with their handiwork.

The Victorians loved to devise elaborate schemes to disguise the features of a room and to embellish or adorn some dull object until it was no longer recognizable. One Victorian innovation was the floral fire screen. There were two varieties of these screens: one was made of mirror covered with dried ferns glued in a pattern to the surface, the other was a form of lattice entwined with dried ivy and enlivened with sprays of pampas grass. Many a farm woman made ''farmer's wreaths'', a collection of seeds, pods, burrs, teasels and other weeds found on the farm. It was made into a circle, wreath, or horseshoe shape and mounted and framed under glass. Collections of dried materials were massed under bell jars or arranged in glass cases. These collections not only ornamented a room, but also provided a study of the local wild plants.

Another idea the Victorians had was to take specimen leaves and flowers, and press them in heavy books. When dry, they were removed and sandwiched between waxed paper, then pressed with a warm iron to melt the wax and coat the leaf. These specimens were either framed as pictures or mounted in a collection book.

Sometimes leaves or sturdy flowers were dipped in melted wax that had been thinned with a little turpentine. This made the plant material heavy but cleanable and quite durable.

From the Victorian era have come books with elaborate and intricate recipes on how to preserve flowers, how to skeletonize leaves and what to do with the finished product. One fad was to embalm the floral work from a dear departed's funeral. This involved taking the arrangement apart, petal by petal, after making a master diagram. After an extremely long and complicated treatment, they were then re-assembled to form the original flower. Flowers bleached, preserved, and waxed in this way kept their whiteness and shape indefinitely. If colour was desired, the petals were tinted with paints before laminating with wax.

Phantom bouquets were another Victorian method of preserving plant material. The art of preparing the fibrous skeletons of plants was practiced by the Chinese many centuries ago. However, it was not a common hobby with the Victorians, since it was a long, tedious procedure (worse than the embalming), and the chance of failure at the end was high. Through a procedure that took months to complete, skeletons of leaves were preserved in much the same way as flower petals.

Flowers were also preserved in drying agents as well. Fine silver sand with pulverized alum and plaster of Paris was a good mixture for keeping white flowers white. Other agents included cornstarch, powdered sugar, fuller's earth, powdered pumice, salt, borax, sand and corn meal. Varying degrees of success were obtained from these mixtures, but nothing was as simple or as satisfactory as the silica gel method is today.

Also from *The Popular Art Instructor*, this illustration shows the preserved skeletons of leaves.

A round mass arrangement in a rice bowl: preserved delphinium, snapdragons, yellow daisies, mock orange, dusty miller, and pressed maidenhair fern.

Chapter 4 Tips on Growing and Harvesting
by Patricia Morgan, O.D.H.

The most rewarding way to preserve flowers is to follow a plant through from start to finish, from selecting the seed to placing the dried flower in an arrangement. There is no time of year that does not lend itself to working in one way or another with plants that can be preserved, and the work need not be limited to harvesting and preserving.

Because started plants of flowers suitable for preserving are not available from the average bedding plant grower, these plants must be raised from seed at home. Occasionally, started plants of strawflowers or statice may be purchased, but very few others are available.

Ordering Seed for Air-Dried Plants

Seed catalogues are mailed immediately after Christmas. Make sure that you receive them, so that while last year's blooms adorn the table, you can make plans for the coming year. Usually most catalogues have a section labelled ''Everlasting''. Here the usual flowers for drying are listed, but not the grasses; and, as often as not, plants that produce interesting seed pods are missing too. The best policy is to read the catalogues from cover to cover, in order to discover new material that is worth trying, which makes the business of growing flowers for drying so exciting. Descriptive phrases such as ''chaffy flower heads'', ''interesting seed pods'' and ''suitable for winter decoration'' are enticing, and they connote plants that are well worth a try. Personal garden problems such as soil types, weather, and climatic conditions must be kept in mind, as well the hardiness of the new plants, and whether they are annual or perennial. With the aid of a greenhouse, if you are fortunate enough to have one, growing seasons can be lengthened, and some perennials that are not hardy can be induced to flower the first year or perhaps even last the winter to bloom again.

When the description of the plant material is not too clear, or when the plant is completely unknown, it is a good idea to read the catalogue with a gardeners' dictionary at hand. Two excellent reference books are *Taylor's Encyclopedia of Gardening* (1957) by Norman Taylor, and *Taylor's Guide to Garden Flowers* (1958), published by Houghton Mifflin, Boston. Seeds may be listed under different names in various catalogues, so it is a good idea to make a cross reference to avoid a duplication of order. There may be several species of flowers in the ''everlasting'' class belonging to the same botanical genus as a number of different, although related, flowers, and all of them may be worth trying.

The cost of seed, no matter how high priced a packet may be, is slight compared with the time, trouble, cost of fertilizers, soil preparation and other items that are required to have a successful crop. It doesn't pay to skimp on a few pennies. Buy from reputable dealers where you believe you will receive top-quality, fresh, true-to-name seed.

Seeds from abroad take a very long time to arrive in Canada. It is wise to order in the fall for spring requirements. Even when letters and the seed are posted air mail, the delays are unbelievable. Some seeds are subject to customs inspection and import regulations, which cause further delays. And when the long-awaited answer finally arrives and you are checking the seed against the invoice, you may discover that substitutions have been made or, for no apparent reason, a selection is missing and a duplication of another one is enclosed, or an unrelated variety is substituted. Another disadvantage of ordering from abroad is that some seeds are unable to stand the fluctuating temperatures they may encounter while in transit, and they germinate poorly on arrival.

Seeds require special storing if they are not to be sown immediately. A copper container such as a biscuit tin makes an ideal storage box for seed. Most seeds should be stored in an atmosphere of low humidity and temperatures from 45° to 50°F. The new foil packets help to keep seeds fresher longer. Do not open a fresh pack of seed until it is time to plant it. The longer the seeds are stored, the lower the viability.

Staking to encourage the growth of curved stems.

18

Growing Plants for Air-Drying

Growing flowers and grasses for drying is no different than for any other purpose. All plants need care and attention to meet their particular requirements. They must be watered, fed and cultivated, and if grown out of their natural habitat, conditions must be maintained similar to those in which they grew naturally, in order to get good results.

Pests must be watched for and controlled. The Tarnish Beetle can sting strawflowers so badly that no bloom will appear; the plant seems to go to leaf. "Yellows" can also ruin a strawflower crop. Aphids are a pest on *Acroclinium* and *Rhodanthe*, sucking the juices from the plants, causing colourless, misshaped flowers. When the plants are very tiny, a crop can be ruined by any number of pests, including diseases, grubs, bugs, beetles and ground hogs.

Disbudding of a plant will produce fewer but larger blooms. Allow the main flower stem to shoot up and remove all lateral flower buds from the bottom up. If, however, more and smaller flowers are needed, merely pinch out the tip of the growing seedling when it has attained three to five true leaves, or pairs of leaves. This will encourage the development of side branches on the lower parts of the stem. Usually a bud will start in each leaf axil.

Tall, upright plants will need staking to keep them from falling over during storms and to keep their stems straight, with the flower heads out of the mud. In flower arranging, a curved branch is always interesting, but there is a limit to the number you can use. When the flower heads are downed by storms, moisture can penetrate into the flower buds without a chance to evaporate. The results can be rotted flower buds or diseases such as mildew or botrytis. Careless watering by hose or sprinkler can cause the same problem, so ground-soaking is better than over-head sprinkling. Crowded conditions in the flower bed, be it from over-ambitious planting or competition from weeds, can ruin late summer harvesting. As the days shorten, and dew remains longer on the plants, botrytis sets in and flower buds rot.

Disbudding at the top to encourage small blossoms at the sides.

Harvesting Plants for Air-Drying

Harvesting plant material for drying and preserving can be a year-round pursuit. As soon as the first flowers appear, the harvest has started. There is never much colour in a dried-flower garden, because as soon as a flower reaches its peak, it is cut. If the garden ever becomes colourful, it means the gardener is either ill or absent.

In general, material for drying should be cut after the dew is off, on a clear day of low humidity. Since dried material shrinks considerably, cut more than is needed. Blossoms are best cut as soon as they have opened: mature blooms do not dry satisfactorily, and buds do not always open properly.

Harvesting Plants for Preserving

Whether you are cutting from your own garden, collecting wild plant material or buying from a florist, there is one important fact to remember: *The flowers must be in top condition*. Since the best results are obtained when flowers are at their peak, the ideal flowers to preserve are the ones from your own garden. You can cut your flowers and put them into the drying material immediately, as soon as they reach their peak, if the conditions are right. It is preferable to pick on a dry sunny day. Late afternoon is the best time, after the morning dew has dried off and before the evening dew falls. Never pick after a rain; wait at least a day, or until the flowers have a chance to dry. The flowers must be free of excess moisture before burying them in the silica gel. Shake them gently, head down, and this will help to remove any drops of rain. Wipe them lightly with a facial tissue.

Pick only a few flowers at a time, selecting them with care. Use only the ones in perfect condition and pick them just before the height of their bloom. Any blemish will show up in the drying. Flowers, particularly roses, which have a tight hard bud in the centre are difficult to process, because the crystals must be able to penetrate among the petals. That hard little bud will not dry at the same time as the rest of the flower, if ever, and it may ruin a whole box of flowers when they are stored.

If it is not possible to process the flowers immediately after picking, place them in water to prevent wilting, because it is essential that the flowers be fresh and crisp in order to dry satisfactorily. When picking from a garden, take a container of water with you and put the flowers into it as soon as they are picked. Water should never be icy cold; lukewarm water is recommended, except for tulips — they like cool water. All flowers and foliage that exude a milky substance should be burnt at the end of the stems as soon as they are picked. This treatment is also necessary for poppies.

After putting the flowers in the lukewarm water, promptly place the container in a cool, dark place and let stand for at least two hours, or overnight, to harden. This procedure is essential for garden flowers, wildflowers and for purchased ones. It is not necessary to do so if you are preserving immediately after picking.

Specific handling instructions for certain flowers will be given in Chapter Ten.

Susanna Moodie painted this bouquet of cut garden flowers in 1869. Courtesy of the Royal Ontario Museum, Toronto.

Chapter 5   Winter Bouquets from Wildflowers
by Dorothy E. Swales

Anemone *(Anemone canadensis)*

Bleuet *(Houstonia caerulea)*
From *Wild Flowers of Canada*, published by *The Montreal Star* in the 1890's.

Desmond Morris tells us in *The Human Zoo* that much of the erratic and even violent behavior of the present day stems from living in crowded concrete jungles, away from the things of the earth. Even if no personal pressures are felt from the twentieth-century way of life, any sensitive person has within him the need for natural beauty in his surroundings.

Summer is relatively brief in Canada except on the west coast, and although snow has its own beauty, we tend to revel in memories of scents and colour which break the monotony of the winter landscape. The material needs of many families, or the lighting and plan of their particular dwellings, as well as their fast-paced, busy lives, may prevent them from growing house plants or buying cut flowers. For such people a new door has opened to a method involving very low cost. The process of drying of wild plants has been perfected so that they can be perserved in their original shape and colour for winter bouquets. The door is open to anyone who loves the outdoors and has the opportunity to walk along a country road, or search for treasure in the hedgerow of an old pasture. Most preservation has been done with garden flowers in the past, but the field is wide open now for experimentation with wildflowers.

Biologists are constantly stressing the need for conservation of our environment now that the effects of over-picking, spraying, and development have become glaringly obvious, and the flowers we knew in picnic spots as children have thinned out or disappeared. The drying and preserving of wildflowers helps us to get acquainted with a form of life that is gradually diminishing, as long as we are careful to pick only those that will not suffer from our treasure hunts.

There are many types of flowers which are aggressive, which reproduce bountifully, and which may be picked, within reason, without any damage to the environment. These include many widespread Canadian plants which originated in Europe and Asia, and arrived with the pioneers, as precious potted plants, as impurities in a package of seed or in a bag of grain, as ballast thrown out of a boat, or even in the cuffs of pants worn trudging through a flowery meadow in Europe and emptied on the ground in Canada.

An introduced plant lacks the same competition that it had at home and often goes on a rampage in the new host country; the orange hawkweed is a prime example. Many attractive flowers of Europe and Asia may be known as weeds in Canada, but they still deserve the time required to dry and preserve them for the winter.

The line drawings appearing in this chapter are reproduced from Roger Peterson's *A Field Guide to Wildflowers of Northeastern and North-central North America*, courtesy of Houghton Mifflin Company, publishers.

21

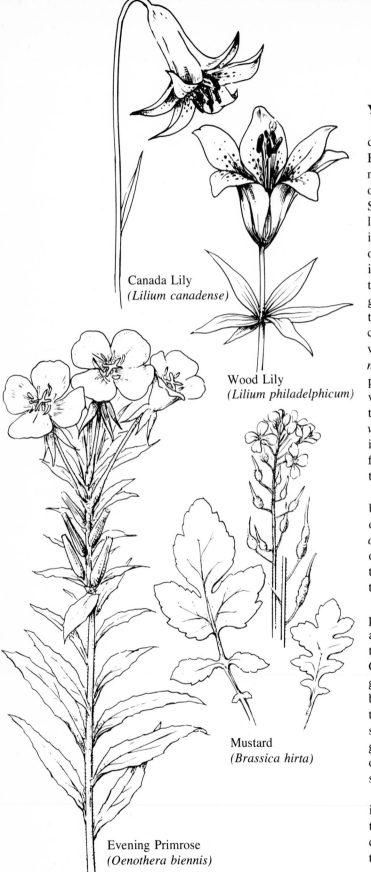

Canada Lily
(*Lilium canadense*)

Wood Lily
(*Lilium philadelphicum*)

Mustard
(*Brassica hirta*)

Evening Primrose
(*Oenothera biennis*)

Yellow to Orange Flowers

Anyone who has gone for a late spring or early summer drive through farmlands anywhere from Newfoundland to British Columbia must have exclaimed at golden-yellow masses of flowers in grain fields or on the roadsides, progeny of some of our most successful immigrants, the mustards. Some species, like *Brassica hirta* and *Brassica juncea*, bloom legitimately on the Prairies as well-bred varieties devoured in the form of the yellow condiment smeared on hot dogs or hidden in salami. But most varieties are unwelcome intruders in our grain fields, and they dry beautifully, so the collector will be doing both herself and the farmer a good turn by collecting them. As a rule yellow flowers keep their colour well during the drying process and the mustards can be supplemented by buttercups (*Ranunculus* sp.), hawkweeds (*Hieracium* sp.), evening primrose (*Oenothera biennis*) and golden beans (*Thermopsis rhombifolia*), the last a prairie flower. All are aggressive types with wide distribution, which can be picked without endangering the survival of the species. A pretty immigrant, butter-and-eggs (*Linaria vulgaris*), has spread from coast to coast, but cannot be included in the list of recommended species because the flowers are too small to fill easily with silica gel, unlike the similar homegrown snapdragon.

You will certainly be tempted by the yellow to orange blooms of the wood lily (*Lilium philadelphicum*), the symbol of Saskatchewan, or those of the Canada lily (*Lilium canadense*) in eastern Canada, but both species are in serious danger from over-picking, and should be left strictly alone to multiply and carry on their cheerful message to generations to come.

Fortunately, there are other yellow flowers which may be picked freely for the winter bouquet, and these need only air-drying: the goldenrods (*Solidago* sp.). (Do not fear that they will bring hay fever, for that myth has been exploded.) Goldenrod is possibly one of the best-known plants of Canada, growing in Frobisher Bay in the Arctic, on the Atlantic beaches, high up in the Rockies, over the Prairies, and in the mild climate of Vancouver Island; these are not all the same species, of course, but all have those unmistakable golden-yellow flowers. Only the ones in the high mountains, or in the Arctic, need protection from extinction. The other species can be picked freely.

Most members of the daisy family, the *Compositae*, grow in open sunny areas, and are widespread in Canada. Perhaps the one most publicized by painters and poets is the ox-eye daisy which appears in great white and yellow masses along the roads by the sea in New Brunswick and Nova Scotia, but unfortunately it cannot be recommended to the flower drier. The white ray petals tend to discolour at the tips and become distinctly less than white.

Large white flowers on the whole tend to turn creamy or dirty-white when dry, and must be second choice for a bouquet. On the other hand, small white flowers like Queen Anne's Lace *(Daucus Carota)* and tall meadow rue *(Thalictrum polygamum)* dry most attractively and possess interesting leaves for pressing as well.

In the rest of the daisy family, the black-eyed Susan *(Rudbeckia hirta)* of the east, and the somewhat similar *Gaillardia* of the west are excellent subjects for drying; but the dainty fleabanes *(Erigeron* sp.) and the sturdy wild asters have not proven to be satisfactory.

Blue to Purple Flowers

Blue is a beautiful colour because it seems to symbolize the sky and sunny days. There are many shades of blue and combinations of blue with red in our Canadian wildflowers, and many related tints can be combined in one arrangement most effectively. Many of our blue flowers are native to Canada, and often they are not competitive types, so one must make sure that they are plentiful before picking. Pick judiciously, selecting one here and one there rather than taking a lot from one patch, which might do serious damage. Roadside plants and those in full sun in old pastures and meadows are more apt to be sturdy and more aggressive than those in shady, moist areas, so these can be picked more freely without endangering the species.

Listed here are those plants with the widest Canadian geographical distribution and with the best probable suitability for drying. Not all of them have been tested in silica gel, and local species must be tried by each experimenter, who should make the results available to others.

In the West, a blue arrangement could start with harebell *(Campanula rotundifolia)*, larkspur *(Delphinium* sp.), or one of the many species of milk vetch *(Astragalus* sp.) or locoweeds *(Oxytropis* sp.) available there, and perhaps these could be combined with a beardtongue *(Penstemon* sp.).

On the Prairies, the silver Psoralea *(Psoralea argophylla)* would certainly be snapped up for its striking silvery leaves, and the delicate mauve and blue prairie crocus *(Anemone patens)*, a flower which dries exceptionally well, would be a first choice. Other flowers might be added, like the pinkish-purple blazing star *(Liatris ligulistylis)* and its later-blooming relative, the dotted blazing star *(Liatris punctata)*, on the Prairies. There are dozens of possibilities in both British Columbia and on the Prairies, and these are merely a few examples of some eye-catching ones.

23

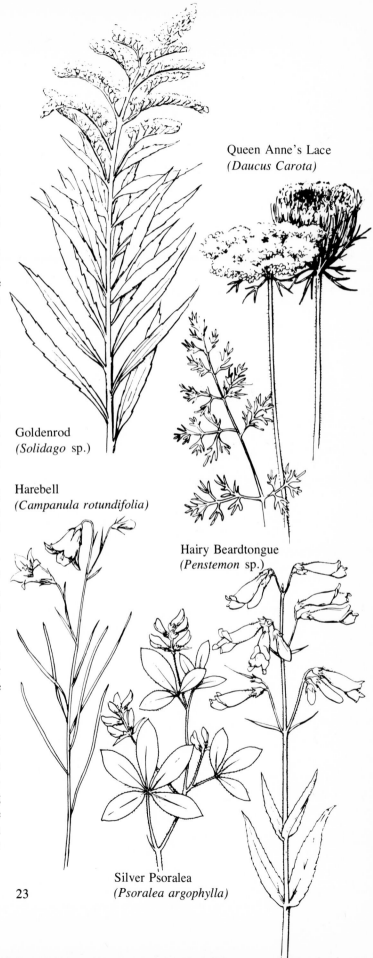

Queen Anne's Lace
(Daucus Carota)

Goldenrod
(Solidago sp.)

Harebell
(Campanula rotundifolia)

Hairy Beardtongue
(Penstemon sp.)

Silver Psoralea
(Psoralea argophylla)

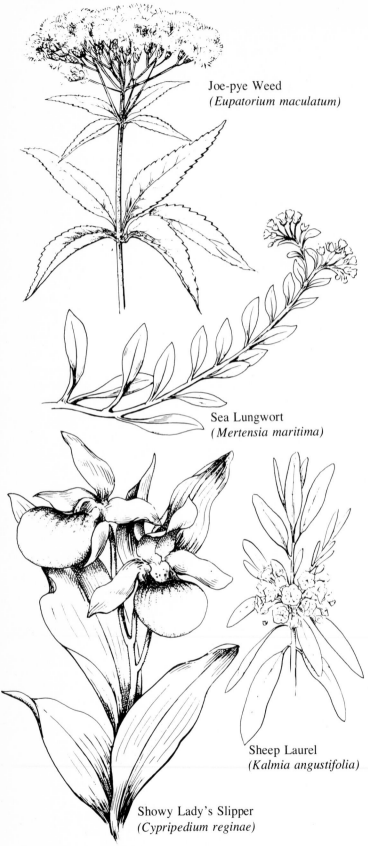

Joe-pye Weed
(*Eupatorium maculatum*)

Sea Lungwort
(*Mertensia maritima*)

Sheep Laurel
(*Kalmia angustifolia*)

Showy Lady's Slipper
(*Cypripedium reginae*)

In the eastern provinces another bellflower (*Campanula rapunculoides*), a frequent and weedy garden escape, lends itself particularly well to drying. You might find blue vervain (*Verbena hastata*), common in moist fields in western and central Quebec and sea lungwort (*Mertensia maritima*) in the beaches of New Brunswick, Nova Scotia and Newfoundland. The common vetch (*Vicia cracca*) and every day clovers (*Trifolium* sp.) make very good subjects for drying, and are always easy to find. Garden lupines, wild and abundant in the Maritimes, would add a riot of blues and purples to the bouquet. Joe-pye weed (*Eupatorium maculatum*) occurs in all provinces, blooms in late summer, and need only be air-dried if picked in the bud stage.

Unfortunately, both fireweed (*Epilobium angustifolium*), common on burnt-over areas, and purple loosestrife (*Lythrum salicaria*), which brings a rosy purple haze over the shores of the St. Lawrence, shrink when dried because of the delicate texture of their petals, and they can't be recommended.

Pink to Red Flowers

Red wildflowers may vary from pale pink, to pink tinged with mauve, and to a deep rose, and include some of our most precious and rare native flowers, the orchids.

We have the pink lady's slipper, (*Cypripedium acaule*), the showy lady's slipper (*Cypripedium reginae*), the fairy slipper (*Calypso bulbosa*), the rose Pogonia (*Pogonia ophioglossoides*), the grass pink (*Calopogon pulchellus*) and a number of others, all shy plants hiding in the shade, and sometimes partially emersed in bog water. None of these should be picked except for scientific purposes, and then with the greatest restraint, for they are among our most beautiful and most easily destroyed wildflowers.

However, there are plenty of widespread and aggressive pink flowering plants available for drying; for example, the flowering rush (*Butomus umbellatus*), which is present over vast areas in shallow water or on the shores of the St. Lawrence River, dries in perfect form. Members of the heather family, or *Ericaceae*, have pink to rose flowers, often bearing a fascinating waxy texture. The sheep laurel (*Kalmia angustifolia*) of the East is bright rose; the bog laurel in all provinces is a delicate pale pink, and the blueberries and cranberries (*Vaccinium* sp.), known across the continent, vary in the intensity of their colour and the waxiness of their flowers.

The queen of pink flowers, the single wild rose, has to be omitted, for its petals tend to fall off so readily it is hard to handle after drying. The smartweeds (*Polygonum* sp.) lack petals, but their pink papery sepals often produce attractive inflorescences which may be air-dried after removing the leaves, which shrivel and become ugly. Those smart-

24

weeds with thick, bright pink spikes which grow either in the water or on very wet shores (*Polygonum amphibium* var. *emersum*) should be picked with caution, since that species is much less aggressive than the others.

Miniatures

A specialized and very fascinating branch of flower-drying is connected with the making of miniature arrangements, which are put in an egg-cup or any other tiny container. There is infinite variation in the small flowers or bits of inflorescences which can be used for this hobby, but the larger-flowered violets, picked in the young stage, as well as twinflowers *(Linnaea borealis)*, bleuets *(Houstonia caerulea)* in eastern Canada, and blue-eyed Mary *(Collinsia grandiflora)* in western Canada, are all good possibilities.

Everlastings

Our generation is not the first one to use winter bouquets, although the new methods of drying discussed here permit much more striking and varied arrangements than our grandmothers ever saw. Most everlastings are so-named because they have dry, papery flower parts, or papery bracts subtending the flowers, and we can do as the pioneers did: hang them upside down in a dry airy place until the stems become rigid. The occasional one, like yarrow *(Achillea Millefolium)* is stiff enough when picked to use immediately. The old-timers loved the pearly everlasting *(Anaphalis margaritacea)*, the French immortelle *(Antennaria* sp.), the sand dock *(Rumex venosus)* on the Prairies, and thrift *(Armeria maritima)* on either coast. If you live within sight of the Atlantic salt marshes you can gather sea lavender or sea heather *(Limonium nashii)*, both of which give pleasure all winter.

Grasses

Our grandparents did not have as much spare time as modern citizens do to search for suitable and original plants for air-drying. We know of many more, particularly from such groups as grasses and sedges. There are the graceful ones which grow in damp spots, like manna grass *(Glyceria* sp.). common cord-grass *(Spartina pectinata)*, an eastern and prairie species, and graceful cord-grass *(Spartina gracilis)* of the Prairies and B.C.; or the cotton grass *(Eriophorum* sp.), a sedge found in bogs, with white or tawny tops, so like a child's tousled head. Dry areas may yield wild barley *(Hordeum jubatum)*, with its long intriguing awns, or grama grass *(Bouteloua gracilis)*, with an oriental look. There are some stiff dune grasses, *Elymus mollis* and *Ammophila breviligulata*, which could add a stark modern touch to an arrangement. All grasses and sedges must be picked in the very early stages or they will shed their spikelets when dried and look a sorry mess among the flowers.

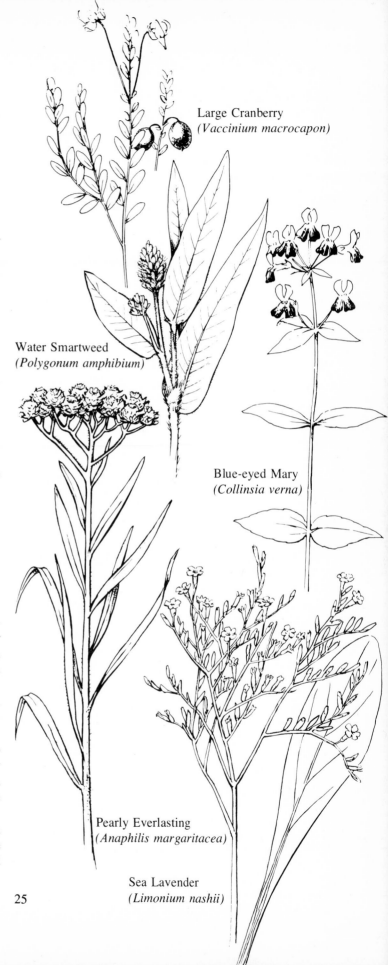

Large Cranberry
(Vaccinium macrocapon)

Water Smartweed
(Polygonum amphibium)

Blue-eyed Mary
(Collinsia verna)

Pearly Everlasting
(Anaphilis margaritacea)

Sea Lavender
(Limonium nashii)

25

Ferns

Ferns have pictorially interesting leaves known as fronds, which seem to fit in a house with primitive paintings and furniture of very plain design. The fronds are broken up into small divisions of great delicacy, called pinnae and pinnules, pleasing to the eye of an artist. They grow mostly in shady woodlands, and so have much suitable space in which to expand in British Columbia and all of eastern Canada. The dry plains are not for them, although some occur along the moister borders of the prairie provinces. They can be prepared for winter bouquets by first pressing them between folds of newspapers, interspersed with sheets of corrugated cardboard cut from cartons, to allow the free circulation of air; then putting them in a warm dry place with a board and weight on top. The original newspapers should be changed to fresh ones within two days and any crooked pinnae should be straightened out while they are still somewhat flexible. When completely dry, they are very brittle and must be handled with extreme care, but they are most effective in both large and small arrangements.

Eastern Canada claims fairly exclusive claim to the royal fern (*Osmunda regalis*), the cinnamon fern (*Osmunda cinnamomea*) and the interrupted fern (*Osmunda claytoniana*), all very handsome large species, but British Columbia has the most spectacular, the sword fern (*Polystichum munitum*). All Canada knows the spinulose shield fern (*Dryopteris spinulosa*) which remains green under the snow during the winter, and most of Canada, except Saskatchewan, has the lady fern *(Athrium Filix-femina)*, which, as the name suggests, is delicately pretty but is forceful enough to push the other ferns aside. Another fern known throughout Canada, which contributes to the economy of New Brunswick, is the ostrich fern (*Pteretis pensylvanica*), which yields the delicious fiddleheads of spring, frozen commercially in New Brunswick; but it is also ready to serve in a dry bouquet. The daintiest of our ferns, the maidenhair (*Adiantum pedatum*) is fairly common in western Quebec and eastern Ontario, but becomes scarce in the Maritimes, reappearing in southwestern Alberta and becoming fairly common again on the west coast and in the Columbia Valley of B.C. In areas where it is plentiful, it is strongly recommended for use in flower arrangements.

Ferns as a rule produce a number of fronds from one root system, so the conservationist should be most particular to take only one frond, or at most two, from a single clump, and pass along to another, rather than strip a single clump of all its powers of rejuvenation.

Bellflower *(Campanula rapunculoides)*

Tall Swamp Thistle *(Cnicus muticus)*
From *Wild Flowers of Canada*, published by *The Montreal Star* in the 1890's.

26

Guidelines on Habitats and Methods of Picking

A good general rule for the flower-picker is to stick to the roadsides, the old pastures and the abandoned meadows in full sunshine to find the sturdiest plants in the least danger of becoming rare or extinct, and except in the case of noxious weeds, to pick individuals here and there, rather than in one spot. River banks and streams are also excellent sources of material, for the same species tend to be repeated over and over along a shore. The woods must be visited for ferns in midsummer or earlier, but the spring flowers there, which spring from bulbs and thickened rhizomes, should be left untouched as a heritage for the coming generation. Trilliums are completely protected by law in Ontario, and should be protected everywhere. Hepaticas, formerly abundant, are now few and far between, as a result of over-picking. Bloodroot could easily be wiped out and dog's-tooth violets, which require at least four years of growth before they can flower, need protection from ruthless hands. The list can be extended *ad infinitum*, so it is important to show suitable restraint and concern for the future of these plants.

When the flower or inflorescence only is going to be used, it can be clipped off in the field with pruning shears and popped into a plastic bag with damp moss or newspaper in the bottom to delay wilting. The leaves will then be left in the field to carry on their work of manufacturing food to store for the next year, in the case of biennials or perennials, and the green covering of the ground will not be marred. Ferns should be put into a large plastic bag quickly after picking and should be pressed as soon as possible after that.

Care should be taken not to leave plastic bag in direct sunlight during transportation, for the ferns will "cook" if this happens.

Guidelines to the Identification of Plants

You will be disappointed with any field guide to the identification of plants, for the species are so numerous, that no small book can cover them all. But Roger Tory Peterson's *Field Guide to Wildflowers of Northeastern and North-central North America*, 1968, and *A Field Guide to the Ferns and their Related Families of Northeastern and Central North America*, 1956 by Broughton Cobb, are both well-illustrated and helpful. *The Flora of Nova Scotia* by A. E. Roland and E. C. Smith, 1969 edition, also has many illustrations and is useful in the Maritimes. In Quebec and eastern Ontario Frère Marie-Victorin's *Flore Laurentienne*, 1964 edition, available in French only, is indispensable. Almost every species in Quebec is illustrated with black line drawings.

The Prairies are well covered in *Wild Plants of the Canadian Prairies*, 1964, by A. C. Budd and K. F. Best, publication 983 of the Canada Department of Agriculture. Representative species are illustrated and all species are described in terms easily understood by the amateur botanist.

Two small inexpensive booklets, *The Ferns and Fern Allies of British Columbia*, 1956, by T. M. C. Taylor, handbook No. 12, and *The Heather Family of British Columbia*, 1962, by Adam Szczawinski, handbook No. 19, are available from the British Columbia Provincial Museum, each species illustrated. All the plants of the northwest zone of B.C. are described and illustrated in detail in five volumes of *The Vascular Plants of the Pacific Northwest* by Hitchcock, Cronquist, Ownbey and Thompson, published between 1955 and 1969, but these books are rather expensive and may be consulted in the libraries of the B.C. universities or at the provincial museum at Victoria.

If book aids prove inadequate, the identifications of plants can be obtained by sending them, carefully packaged to avoid shattering, to any institutes which have a collection of pressed plants in a herbarium. Such centres are: the Provincial Museum of B.C., Victoria, B.C.; the National Museum of Natural Sciences, or the Department of Agriculture at the Central Experimental Farm, both in Ottawa, Ontario; or the Departments of Botany at any of our large Canadian universities. The university nearest your area would be best, since that one is more apt to specialize in local plants. Herbaceous plants sent for identification should include root, stem, some leaves, and either the inflorescence or the fruit, as any or all of these parts may be necessary for identification. Such plants should be collected in duplicate, a number given to each pair, and one of the pair sent away and the other retained by the sender. Then the duplicate can be offered to the institution in return for the service given, and the name of the plant only, opposite the given number, returned to the sender. This is a standard procedure, unless the plant is rare.

A round centrepiece made of preserved tulips, globe flowers, star of Bethlehem, foxglove, mock orange, and pressed maidenhair fern.

Chapter 6 Preserving Flowers with Silica Gel by Roy and Anne Boake

With the aid of new products and processes, it is now possible to create dried flower arrangements and designs that last a long time and preserve most of the original beauty of the natural material. One of the prime factors in the new method is the use of silica gel.

Silica gel is a chemical compound which has been used in industry for many years because of its ability to absorb large quantities of moisture. More recently, it has found acceptance as a drying medium for flowers. In 1961, Mrs. Dorothea Thompson published an article in American Home magazine about her use of silica gel for the drying of flowers, and as a result it was put on the market by a large chemical company. The special mixture for flower-drying includes an added blue crystal indicator.

Other Methods of Preserving Plants

There are a number of dehydrating agents that have been used for drying plant material and some are still in use. Sand alone is one that has been used over the years. There are records of it being used in ancient Egyptian times, and in the fourteenth and fifteenth centuries and, at times, it has been combined with other materials. Using it alone, or in conjunction with other ingredients, the sand has to be carefully prepared. It must be sifted to remove any foreign matter, washed and then dried in the sun or oven. If it is too coarse, it will pock mark the flowers. "Play box" sand has been used with fairly good results. However, it requires about three weeks to dry the flowers by the sand method. In areas where the growing season is short, you must have a great deal of sand on hand to catch all your flowers in their prime. Another disadvantage is the weight of the sand, which puts considerable strain on the delicate petals.

Another dessicant, borax, is fast-drying, making the timing difficult to determine. Flowers dried too long turn brown and bleach. For this reason, borax is sometimes mixed with sand or cornmeal, which tends to roughen its texture. A disadvantage of both combinations is that the flower emerges from the mixture with a white coating plainly visible on the surface of the petals, which is difficult — sometimes impossible — to remove.

The Advantages of Silica Gel

Because of the many drawbacks of these older methods, they have been discarded by many people in favour of silica gel. It requires no preliminary preparation except thorough drying. It leaves no dusty residue that cannot be cleaned off, with perhaps one exception. Flowers that have a sticky surface, like petunias, do not clean easily, but petunias, except for the double ones, are unsatisfactory flowers for drying.

The silica gel and blue crystal mixture is coarse enough

29

to make it stable, and fine enough to run into the fine limits between petals so that all surfaces are in contact with the material, since it is essential for the flowers to be completely buried in the mixture.

Silica gel for flower-drying is readily available in the United States at most florists' and garden supply centres. In Canada, it can be bought through only a few centres. A list of suppliers appears in Chapter Ten.

Preparing the Silica Gel

Although silica gel is quite expensive, it does not deteriorate and may be used and re-used almost indefinitely. The blue crystal indicators in the silica gel fade to a pinky-beige when it has absorbed all the moisture it can hold. It can be dried and used again by placing it in a 250° oven in a pan or cookie tin. When the crystal indicators turn blue again, the mixture is dry. It is, of course, faster if you use a large shallow pan.

Stir the silica gel occasionally while it is heating. When it is dry, let it cool in an airtight container before using it again, as the hot silica gel will burn the flowers. *The importance of keeping the silica gel dry cannot be over-emphasized*. The crystal indicators *must* be bright blue when the dessicant is used or the results will be disappointing.

Silica gel is light in weight and easy to handle. Most flowers will dry in approximately three days; some take more time, some less. The lightness of the mixture and the quick drying time allows the flower to emerge from the silica gel retaining most of its natural beauty and colour.

Step by Step Procedure

All equipment, silica gel, and containers should be collected in a good working area. This may be in any convenient area in your home where you have good daylight or strong artificial light. It is important to have a tray on which you can do all the covering and uncovering of the flowers, in and out of the containers. This way you will prevent the scattering of the silica gel and will avoid wastage.

Equipment needed: sharp knife or scissors (never use dull instruments in cutting flowers); wire clippers; secateurs for heavy branches; green florist's wire in various gauges — #18 for thick stems, #23, average weight for wiring, #26 lighter, and #30 fine wire for very delicate flowers; wooden pick or toothpicks; florist's tape (a stretchy waxed roll of narrow paper used for covering wire stems, in two shades of green and brown); white and green masking tape (also knows as Oasis tape); and freezer tape for sealing containers for storage, etc. Cellophane tape is apt to dry out and lift off so it is not recommended. Also a soft paint brush for cleaning flowers; tweezers for delicate work; clear adhesive to replace or reinforce petals; plastic spray; facial tissues; and a box of silica gel.

The necessary containers are cake and cookie tins, plastic ice cream containers, coffee tins, tall juice tins, and long boxes. Any kind of container can be utilized that is leakproof and of sufficient size so that your flowers are not crowded. For storage until flowers are arranged, large plastic boxes can be used if they can be properly sealed so that they are airtight.

The next step is to choose a container for the particular flower you are going to preserve. Some flowers are round, others are trumpet-shaped or clustered, others spiked. The important thing is to have a large enough container so that the flower can be completely covered by the silica gel. For a flower such as a deep trumpet-shaped lily, it is necessary to have a deep container. For a spiky flower, use a long narrow box with supports as illustrated on page 38. Usually you can put more than one flower in the box, but it is advisable to restrict each container to one variety. See page 36.

It is necessary to remove the stem of the flower, leaving a section about one inch long extending from the calyx, depending on the flower; allow enough for easy handling. The reason for removing the stem is twofold; it makes for easy handling when burying in the silica gel, and most stems dry at a different rate than the flowers. They are either too brittle for handling in arrangements, or they would take far too long to thoroughly dry out. It would be nearly impossible to dry flower and stem together without a very complicated system, though it can be done in the case of spiky flowers and some flowering shrubs. Details appear on page 38, in the description of the horizontal position and the upright position; and on page 48, under "Drying with Glycerine".

A collection of natural stems can be air-dried separately; i.e. the black-eyed Susan stem can be air-dried and used with any preserved flower in place of a wire stem. The leaves and stems of roses may be preserved in glycerine and combined with a rose that has been preserved in silica gel.

Start by putting a bed of silica gel in the bottom of a container. The depth of this will depend on the specific flower being dried since some will require more than others. The container should be large enough to allow about an inch of silica gel around the flower.

Insert a piece of wire up the stem as far as the calyx or seed pod of the flower, leaving about an inch protruding from the end of the short stem. As the stem dries and shrinks, the wire is secure in the stem and cannot fall out or be readily pulled out. It is important to insert the wire before drying because it cannot be done later. After the flower is dry and you are ready to arrange the flowers, another wire is attached to the short piece to make an artificial stem. The weight of wire used depends on the diameter of the stem.

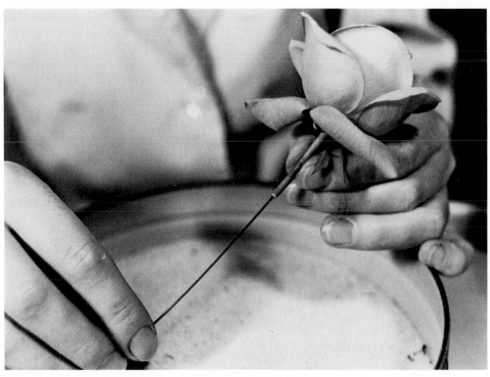

Horizontal or cross-wiring. Sometimes it is impossible to insert a wire up the stem of a flower because of its tough, hard core. This is also the case when the stem is too slim and delicate. The wire is inserted through the calyx, holding the stem in one hand near the calyx. With a tougher calyx, use a heavier wire; with a delicate calyx use a lighter gauge wire.

When cross-wiring is necessary, the wire is folded down, parallel to the stem on each side.

The hook method should be avoided except in a few cases, even though previous publications suggested this method only. The system employs a tiny hook at the top of the wire, with the other end inserted down through the face of the flower into the stem, pulling the wire well down so that the hook is inserted firmly into the centre of the flower. The reason why this method is not recommended is because in the daisy (disk) type of flower, the hook is apt to shatter and destroy the disk. Another reason is that the wire is likely to show when the flower is dry, since there is always a little shrinkage. However, the method is useful with zinnias because they have a thick hollow stem and, in the drying, the calyx or the stem often fails to hold the wire firmly. It is also used in wiring small-stemmed trumpet-like flowers, i.e. freesia, when a very fine wire is used. Special wiring of a few difficult flowers is described in Chapter Ten.

When the flower is wired, bend the wire at a right angle to the stem so that it will sit upright on the bed of silica gel. Flowers should be placed face up whenever possible. At no time is it advisable to bury a disk (daisy-type) flower face down. The silica gel must be worked in between the petals; if the flower is face down, the flower is distorted and has a flattened appearance. The flower should be kept as level as possible. If it is positioned at an angle or lying on its side, there is the danger of deformity and loss of natural shape.

Start covering or burying the flower. Take a handful of silica gel and gradually let it flow along the inside edge of the box away from the flower. Tip the container gently, if necessary, to get the silica gel well under the calyx. Care must be taken not to disturb the flower. Let the silica gel flow gently from your hand.

35

In the case of multiple-petalled flowers, i.e. zinnias, lift the petals of the flowers up with a thin stick so the silica gel penetrates well in between the petals.

This container is filled with as many flowers of one kind as it is possible to get in without crowding or overlapping. It is not *always* necessary to keep to one type of flower per container: flowers that dry at about the same speed can be placed together in the same container.

36

Covering the flowers, continue covering until the box is full and the flowers are completely covered.

You can lift the container up in one hand, gently tap the sides, and the sand will sift down, filling up any air pockets. If tops of flowers again appear, continue covering.

The horizontal position. This is the method best suited to long sprays such as delphinium, mock orange, larkspur, deutzia, etc., which can be done in a long narrow box. Have three pieces of cardboard ready which are the same width as the box but lower in height. Cut a deep notch in the centre top of each piece and place them in the box as illustrated, braced against the sides with the bottom imbedded in the silica gel base. The stock will rest on the support, allowing the lower florets to hang freely above the bed of sand. If care is taken in adding the silica gel, the shape of the floret will not be spoiled by flattening. Start from the outside edge, allowing the silica gel to flow from your hand toward the flowers, distributing it evenly in the middle and along the sides. Work carefully on the lower florets, using a pointed stick to manipulate a stubborn floret. As you cover each flower, shift the stream of silica gel alternately from front to back, to prevent distortion. Maintain the steady flow of silica gel until the spray is covered.

Flowers can also be done in an upright position. This is useful for some sprays and particularly for hyacinths. Again, make a good bed of silica gel, hold the tip of the flower so that the stem is in an upright position, and fill in and around the flower until completely buried.

Trumpet-shaped flowers such as daffodils, tulips, lilies, etc., must be covered with particular care. To preserve the contour and to avoid splitting the petals, place the flower on the bed of silica gel; build up from the outside of the container towards the flower. Never fill the cup first of all. Build up outside the cup a little, then inside, keeping the levels equal on both sides. Continue alternating the flow of silica gel until the flower is covered. By the time you have reached the top, the pressure on the inside and outside should be the same.

Cover and seal the container and label it with the name of the contents, the date, and time of day. Flowers take from two to five days to dry in silica gel. Sometimes weather conditions make a difference, so it is a good idea to make a note on the sealed container if the weather has been particularly damp or humid. Recommended drying times will be given in Chapter Ten. Keep careful records of times and results, in order to guarantee success.

To uncover the flowers, after the period of drying is over, hold the container in one hand and slowly tip it to the side, allowing the silica gel to fall into another container. Be sure to have a tray under the entire work area in order to catch any spill. Pour slowly and steadily; hold the other hand, with second and third fingers spread apart, over the edge of the container as the silica gel is poured, to prevent flowers from falling out and being damaged.

As the flowers appear, keep the container tipped and put two fingers under the flower for support. Continue to let the crystals run off the flower, gently lifting it back and away from the silica gel.

If you feel any dampness in the petals or in the stem or calyx, do not remove any more flowers for a few more days. Roses are tricky. The petals will dry much faster than the calyx. If the calyx is not dry, place the rose or flower on top of the silica gel until it is completely dried. The dry, hard calyx is what holds the flower together, so it is essential that it is thoroughly dried. If one flower with any dampness in it is stored with other flowers, you can easily lose the whole box of flowers.

When you remove a flower from the silica gel, holding it by the stem, turn the flower upside down to allow silica gel between the petals to fall away. Tap the back of your hand gently as shown.

If any further particles of silica gel adhere to the flowers, they can be gently cleaned off by brushing with a camel hair paint brush.

Sometimes it is necessary to replace a petal. Use any glue that is clear when dried, or clear nail polish, diluted in a solution of two parts polish to one part non-oily polish remover.

It is sometimes advisable to reinforce petals by dropping glue on the underside of the petal and by dropping very small drops in between the petals in the case of double flowers. It is wise to do the repairs or reinforcing before storing the flowers. Reinforce such flowers as cosmos and daisies, and the outer petals of roses, especially the single ones. Let the glue dry for five minutes before storing. *Warning: Diluted glue is for reinforcing only. Use undiluted glue when replacing fallen petals.*

Preserved flowers must be stored away from moisture. Flowers dried during the summer must be stored until the weather is dry and cool.

Flowers should be stored in plastic containers, covered and sealed with saran wrap or plastic. Flowers and foliage dried in silica gel or sand, or any dehydrating mixture, will pick up moisture in humid weather and must be protected by proper storage. Tin and plastic containers are the best, but cardboard is not recommended. Put a few tablespoons of dry silica gel in the bottom of the box. Shredded waxed paper can be put in the bottom to make a base on which the flowers can rest; or use a piece of styrofoam; or dry pieces of floral foam, a commercial block of flower-holding material, into which the wired stem of the flower can be stuck to keep it in an upright position. If flowers are laid down carefully and not overcrowded, no holder is necessary. You may wish to store some of your prize blooms separately. When doing so, be sure to have a wide enough container so the blossom can be removed easily.

Always put your fingers underneath the flower to lift it.

If you must use a cardboard box for long sprays, be sure it is sealed at all joins. All containers must be put away in a dry place. Few basements are dry enough for storage. If you live in an apartment, store the container on a shelf in a clothes cupboard. Attics are excellent places, if you have one, or a top-floor cupboard will do if you do not.

A plastic spray can be used to protect the flowers from moisture, but it dries and browns the edges of the petals. They look very good when first sprayed — it seems to brighten the flowers; but as soon as it dries, the flowers appear to be duller. However, if you are going to store your flowers over a second summer, it is advisable to spray them.

After arrangements have been made, arrangements of preserved flowers may be stored for the summer in dark plastic bags with a handful of silica gel sprinkled inside each bag.

Dried and preserved flowers decorate the house during the autumn, winter and early spring. During the time of year when fresh garden blooms or wildflowers are available, dried flowers are not necessary and often are an eyesore. You can freshen them up with a spray as mentioned before, or hair spray. With the everlasting type of flowers, you can steam them by holding them over the spout of a boiling kettle. Even the silica-gel-dried flowers, especially the double variety, can stand a quick swish through the steam. Don't try it with daffodils, narcissus or tulips.

Important

If you are doing a great deal of preserving with silica gel, it is advisable to wear a mask; a surgical mask is the best. Though silica gel is harmless, any inhalation of grain particles can be harmful if done regularly and in the presence of large quantities of gel.

This arrangement of air-dried flowers includes strawflowers, lonas, hairy oats, globe amaranth, and bittersweet preserved in glycerine, in an asymmetrical triangle design.

Chapter 7   Air-Drying and the Glycerine Method
by Patricia Morgan, O.D.H.

The first flowers that you harvest for air-drying usually have short stems, and often not enough of them are ready at once to make up a standard bunch. When you have enough, these are made into mixed bunches for small arrangements. The flowers are bundled with 20-25 stems per bunch, depending on the material. The heads are kept together and the stem length is adjusted when the bunch is tied.

When harvesting, scissors or knife are both satisfactory for cutting, but the knife must be sharp and must cut clean, or else there is a tendency to pull the plant, loosening the hold of the root in the soil. As the bloom is cut, all foliage is stripped from the stem to hasten the drying process. This is quickly accomplished by running the thumb and fingers down the stem of the flower.

The bunches of flowers are then tied securely. As stems lose their moisture they shrink in size, and unless tied securely, they often loosen enough to slip out. Elastic bands or twist-ties are more effective than string to keep materials together. Many bunches of flowers are cut at one time and left lying in the shade until a sufficient load warrants a trip to the drying room.

Flowers for air-drying do not wilt readily. The drying room can be a closet, attic, barn, garage, or any structure, as long as it is in a dry, airy location and can be darkened.

The majority of cultivated and wild plants can be dried by the simplest of all drying methods: hanging upside down. Through the years, this technique of dehydration has been, and still is, the traditional way to dry plants. Our colonial ancestors used this method; old pictures show material neatly bunched and suspended over a kitchen mantle or from a rafter. Today the tobacco industry employs this same principle for its crop. The drying room should be equipped with racks for suspending the bunches of flowers. Nails driven in rafters at regular intervals, or a clothes-drying rack, or clothes-line strung across the room, all are suitable for suspending the bunches. Care must be taken not to pack the flowers too closely, or the drying process will be slowed. Free circulation of air is essential. The plant material should not be covered, shut up in a tight closet, or exposed to direct sunlight while drying. Additional heat speeds up drying but can also be detrimental to colours.

The basic principle of any drying process is the removal of moisture. Plant materials will not last indefinitely if they are only partly dry, and they must be thoroughly devoid of moisture to remain in good condition. In eight to ten days the majority of plants are dry, but weather conditions at the time of drying will govern the number of days required.

While they are drying, plants go through various stages

45

of limpness; when completely dry, plants will be stiff to the touch and the stems will snap easily. Some plant material dries better in an upright position with blooms at the top, particularly those with clustered heads on fine stems; i.e. babies' breath and Joe-pye weed. The natural softness and fluffiness of the sprays is preserved. Cattails, dock, oats, many grasses, and *Xanthiums* all dry satisfactorily if placed upright in a container. Baskets, pails, juice cans and cartons all make excellent containers for drying upright and for storing material completely dried by the upside-down method. Material stored in long florists' boxes tend to crush on one side.

Freezing and thawing does not adversely affect a completely dry plant material, because the moisture has been evaporated out of the plant cells. Dried materials can, however, re-absorb moisture even after a year of drying. *Acroclinium* will close up to bud shape in a moist atmosphere even after being dried for a year, but will reopen if removed to a dry location.

Dried materials can become covered with mildew if they are stored in damp places, and they will completely lose their colour. On the other hand, too dry an atmosphere will cause brittleness and a tendency to shatter. As autumn stretches into winter, the drying room should be watched for over-dry or over-moist conditions and steps should be taken to rectify the situation.

Care should be taken to keep dust from collecting on the plants. A light covering of paper or storage in a tight chamber keeps them fresh longer. Also beware of exhaust fumes from autos or machinery if stored in garages.

Upright air-drying.

46

Wiring

Strawflowers are picked when the first three rows of petals have opened back. The bloom is cut off right below the head and gathered into baskets. The flowers will close. They can be kept for several days before wiring. A #20 wire is inserted into the head, and as the flower dries it reopens and adheres to the wire. Very small strawflowers are impaled on finer wire.

Acroclinium and **Gomphrena** both have a tendency to droop their heads even after they have been thoroughly dried by the hanging method. Both will reabsorb moisture. This can be overcome by placing them on wires as is done for strawflowers. Another method is to strengthen the stem by parallel wiring; place a wire by the stem and bind the two together with florist's tape.

Bunches of flowers hung from a line to air-dry.

Gathering Wildflowers and Grasses

The awns of **bearded wheat** and **barley** tend to stick out all around the head when they are dried. To overcome this problem, a thin paper is tied around the heads of each bunch as it is hung to dry. For best results, the grains must be perfectly dry but immature, and they should be watched for mildew.

Common dock can be picked in three stages. First, when it reaches maturity but is still green; later, during the summer when it has a blush of pinky-rust colour; and finally when it is ripe and rusty-brown.

Larkspur and **delphinium** can be dried by the hanging method quite successfully. Place them upright in a container for two days, and then invert them and hang them for the balance of their drying time. This helps to preserve the shape of the blossom and the form of the flower head.

Thistles are picked just as the centre starts to reopen after forming seed. They are placed upright in a sunny, warm location where they can dry out. Plucking the seeds out speeds up the drying and the opening of the fluffy head.

Rosettes of **mullein** are gathered in the fall. They are pulled or dug out of the ground, and can be made into "roses" by shaping and stuffing each leaf on the plant with facial tissue and drying it that way. A wire twisted around the base or root forms the stem..

Pencil-slim **cattails** are gathered in early summer. More mature ones, if given a spray of varnish, will not burst open.

Most **grains** and **grasses** are picked in their immature green stage to avoid a chaffy look. If dried in the sun, they will have the texture of hay.

Teasels may be picked in their immature green stage, in the brown fall colour, or in late winter when they go almost black.

Since seeds mature at various times of the year, **seed pods** are gathered accordingly. Seed pods are picked at that time in their growth when their size, form and colour are most suitable for decorative effects. Some are best in the immature stage, holding the soft green colour and remaining closed, while others, such as milkweed and thistles, are best when they are fully ripe, with seeds removed.

A garden for dried flowers is not an attractive garden because of continuous harvesting. It can also be a "neglected" garden, because many plants are grown only for their attractive seed cases. A plant gone to seed is not an attractive garden specimen, but it is a delight to the eye of a dried-flower enthusiast.

Cones and **nuts** are also seed cases and they are most attractive in form and colour, not only at Thanksgiving and

Christmas, but all year round. When gathered in their natural habitat, cones often have a sticky substance called "pitch" sticking to them. A vigorous wash in detergent suds with a stiff brush will remove the gum. After washing, the cones may be dried by artificial heat, or spread in a single layer and left outdoors in the shade, as direct exposure to sunlight can impair their natural colour. If dried in the kitchen oven, the heat must be kept low or the colour can be impaired. As the cones dry, the scales open and expand; some cones will almost double their size. A popping and cracking noise usually accompanies the opening of the scales, and if they are dried in the oven, a lovely pine smell permeates the whole house.

Caution: If the oven isn't swept clean of seeds, the next baked goods could be set on fire or could taste of pine.

Fall is the ideal time for gathering nuts, as all squirrels know. But in the winter, after a mild spell, look for a place where a squirrel has had a banquet, and there will be walnut, butternut, and beechnut shells already cracked; also the remains of a cache may be found. Often the shells are as interesting and more useful than the nuts.

To store nuts, wash them in soapy water and lay them out on a flat surface to dry. Leave them exposed to air for a few weeks to dry thoroughly; then they may be stored in a container with a handful of moth flakes to discourage worms and insects. If stored in damp places, mildew can ruin them.

Drying with Glycerine

Some flowers respond to different methods of drying. **Statice** will not become brittle and shatter if it is allowed to drink up a solution of 2 parts water to 1 part glycerine for 48 hours. The colour is not affected in any way, and the branches and flowers stay pliable indefinitely.

Bittersweet branches perform well in the glycerine solution. The leaves become yellow-green, but they remain on the branch. The berries open and remain plump rather than shrivelled, and they do not drop off or lose their colour.

The **leaves and branches** of many of our trees when treated in a glycerine solution will last indefinitely. They are not, in the true sense of the word, dried, since they are not stiff, but rather pliable and very long-lasting; but they are certainly not fresh.

Choose branches which absorb water freely and are fresh and in excellent condition. If there is a time lapse between picking and placing in glycerine solution, revive the branches by placing them in tepid water in a cool, dark location. Branches may be picked at any time, and, depending on age, the leaves will turn various colours in solution. During warm months, they absorb the solution faster, speeding up the process.

Specimen branches are cut no longer than three feet; the base of the stem is slashed or mashed with a hammer for at least one inch to expose a greater surface for absorption. A solution is made of 1 part glycerine to 2 parts water, in a container filled to a depth of 4 inches to 5 inches. Place the stem or branch in the solution and allow it to remain until saturated.

Some leaves reach saturation in a few days, others require weeks. While in the solution, the foliage should never be covered or crowded and should have a free circulation of air. To determine when the branch has reached saturation, an oily slickness on the surface of the leaf can be felt when it is rubbed between the fingers. Some leaves will exude droplets of solution and some will change colour.

Branches which have been processed through the glycerine solution can be used in dried or fresh arrangements; placing the stems in water can do no harm. These leaves last for years and may be used over and over again. If they become dusty or mildewed from poor storage, they can be washed off with warm soapy water.

Pressing

Some **ferns** will absorb the glycerine solution, but it changes their colour to a dirty, mud brown. They can be bleached and dyed later, but this gives them an artificial look and their beauty is lost. Ferns gathered in late summer can be dried by pressing. Their colour softens and the feathery quality of some of them is only diminished by a trifle.

When gathering ferns, don't collect any more than can be handled before they wilt. A basket lined with damp paper helps to retain their freshness, but does not wet their leaves. Large telephone directories make an excellent botanical press, skipping two pages between each specimen. If a large quantity of leaves are to be pressed, roll back a carpet, spread a double layer of papers on the floor in the rug area, carefully arrange a layer of leaves over the papers, then cover with additional papers, then another layer of leaves and more papers and so on. Roll back the rug over the new "under-padding", and the leaves may be stored there indefinitely.

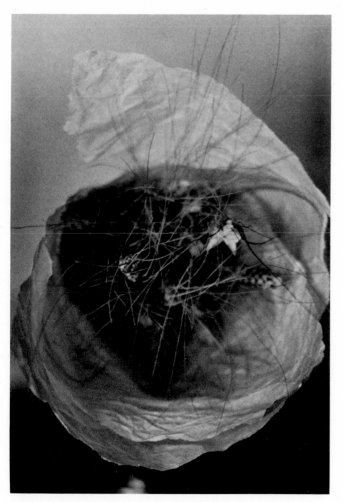

Wheat wrapped in tissue and hung to dry.

This glass slipper contains a line arrangement of clarkia, deutzia, ageratum, pink Sunday salvia and godetia preserved in silica gel.

Chapter 8 Arranging the Flowers
by Dorothy Kimpton

Arranging preserved flowers requires skill and a good deal of patience, as well as knowledge of the basic rules of flower arrangement. There are many good books on flower arrangement, and we do not propose to go into the basic designs in great detail. It is advisable for anyone planning to preserve flowers to take a course on arranging fresh flowers and to read all you can on the subject. You will find yourself collecting books on flower arrangement as some people collect cook books.

The basic rules are the same for dry flowers as they are for fresh ones. Strict rules have been laid down for competitions, and reading a rule book might discourage you from ever attempting any kind of flower arranging. However, you will find that these books simply tell you the basic rules of good design — proportion, balance, harmony, rhythm, and top condition of material. There are some people who see instinctively whether the balance and proportion of an arrangement is right; others need much practice and training before they know for sure. You cannot learn through easy mechanical measurements, or if you do your flower arrangement will look like a paint-by-number picture.

Flower arrangers in the twentieth century have been influenced by the traditional mass arrangements of Europe and the ancient art of linear flower arrangements from Japan, using simplicity of line and only a few branches and flowers. From these two opposite schools arose the typical North-American style, the combination of line and mass. In all arrangements, no matter what school you follow, the basic rules are the same.

Arrangements of flowers are so much a matter of individual taste that we hesitate to lay down hard and fast rules. So much depends on the surroundings and on the furnishings of the room into which the flowers are to go. We will restrict our discussion to useful tips on the special handling of preserved flowers. However, one important thing to remember is that the plant material you are using is part of nature and should look as natural as possible. Some arrangers, particularly in flower shows, are doing interpretive arrangements which often seem to be a far cry from the world of nature.

Choose your container with care. The correct choice is more important for dry than for fresh flowers. The colour and shape of the container must be truly complementary, since the wrong choice is jarring to the eye and detracts from the picture of perfection you are trying to achieve. The arrangement is meant to be enjoyed for many months, and you will not want any little irritating flaws in constant view. Vases with simple shapes and soft colours will always enhance the blooms; they look especially well in pewter and copper, in ceramics of dull black, grey-green, and ivory. Wait until you have some experience before using patterned containers, which can be very effective when used with discretion.

Although they are heavily patterned, lovely cache pots and some Chinese bowls often show subtle colours. Italian and Spanish pottery, even the most coarse and brilliantly coloured, can serve well when there is some relationship between the shape of your flowers and the shape of these pots. But preserved flowers have a more natural look in a container of simple clean lines.

When using formal flowers such as roses and lilies, Lalique glass, silver, gilded materials, porcelain, and alabaster are most often the perfect choices. The choice must not only be in harmony with the flowers, but also with the room in which they are placed. Stately homes containing antiques and fine art demand the finest possible containers, subtle enough to blend softly with their elegant surroundings. For this home, usually the classic or conservative design is the most suitable. However, though roses and lilies may be considered the more formal flowers, they can be used in the simplest containers in the most informal rooms. A copper bowl or a wicker basket filled with a mixture of garden roses can be charming and delightful. A single lily in a narrow-necked ceramic vase or bottle in a room with contemporary furnishings can give more pure delight than the most exotic flowers in the finest crystal.

Copper and pewter are a great foil for the robust zinnas and other sturdy flowers and they work best of all in a casual setting, on a pine chest, an oak table, or painted wood, and in rooms where linen, homespuns, wools and brasses are traditional.

Flowers for bedrooms should be planned according to the furnishings. If it is a very feminine room it will accept delightful porcelian pieces, Dresden china, glass phials, and antique English and French china more gracefully. If there is a masculine influence in the room, untippable arrangements are recommended, to avoid irritation with your decorating endeavours. Let these flowers blend discreetly into the total atmosphere, placing them not so prominently that they will cause a small disaster in a moment of hurry.

Put a tiny basket of dried wildflowers in a child's room for a warm touch, to inspire appreciation and curiosity.

Containers of many varied materials, sizes, and shapes are easily found for the kitchen and recreation room. Wooden bowls, baskets, tinware moulds, old knifeboxes, and salt boxes are attractive and fun to use. Jugs, mugs, jars, and old bottles which pick up a spark of colour from somewhere in the room are good choices, as are stoneware, bean pots and shapely old crocks.

In entrances, foyers, and hallways there are many possible choices. Here again, consider the background and the space available for the arrangement, and the style of furnishing. Toleware, cloisonne, copper, pewter, modern ceramics, and materials which suggest durability seem the most satisfying in these areas.

This picture shows several containers which have been used time and time again and have proven versatile and satisfactory. Start a collection. Look about at home first of all. You will be surprised at what you will find tucked away on a top shelf — a wedding present you thought you would never be able to use, a piece of china put away because of a crack, an old teacup with a handle missing. Chipped or cracked china can be used with dried flowers, hiding the offending crack. You will find many such useful items at rummage sales, on the white elephant tables at bazaars and at country auctions. It is not necessary to haunt expensive antique shops to find pleasing and useful pieces. Look at the vases in our illustration, and in your mind's eye fill each container and place it in a chosen spot, examining the possibilities for each one. Then do it again with different material. Now you can start your arrangements with confidence.

These are the basic mechanical aids: From left to right, moss to cover the mechanical aids; chicken wire, which is crumpled and placed in the opening of a large vase and held in place with masking tape; block floral foam, with cylinder floral foam in front of it, the most satisfactory aid; floral clay and two pin holders.

53

Floral foam is cut to fit the container, usually to its full depth for more security, allowing a slight rise above the lip for easy placement of stems. It is recommended that you always tape across the foam, from side to side, as illustrated, to prevent the foam from springing up with the weight of the arrangement. It is most important that the flower-holding device, no matter what it is, be secured so firmly in the container so that the arrangement can be turned upside-down without disturbing the materials.

To arrange a few flowers in a shallow dish, a pin holder can be used. It should be secured to the bottom of the dish with floral clay, which is like a soft plasticene. Between your hands, roll out a long enough piece to fit around the outside edge of the base of the pin holder. Press it gently on to the base of the pinholder and place it in the position you wish to have it in the dish; press down, securing the holder with the clay.

Chicken wire is useful for holding long stems in tall, deep vases. The plant material, in this case, is likely to be long grasses, weeds, seed pods and branches. To use chicken wire, crumple or fold the wire to size to fit into the neck of the container, and secure it with masking tape. If you are using a clear glass or crystal vase, you can cut a piece of chicken wire the size of the opening, fitting it flat across the top of the opening, and again secure it well with tape. Masking tape is better than cellophane tape, which will dry and lift off.

Pieces of styrofoam board have been used to hold dried flowers, but this method is not recommended, since it is too difficult to pierce the board with delicate, brittle stems. Sand also has been used to fill containers, and sometimes hot wax has been poured over the top of the sand to secure it in the container. Neither of these methods is as good as floral foam, which is by far the best holder. Foam that has been soaked in water in a fresh flower arrangement does not hold stems as well as a new piece of foam. Once it has been wet, it crumbles more easily.

One of the most important rules in flower arranging is that the mechanical aids must not show in the finished arrangement. The next step is to cover whatever holder you are using. In this arrangement, the foam is covered with a piece of moss. Cover the foam neatly, trimming the edges of the moss and tucking it well down around the foam. It can be held in place by pinning it down with hairpin-shaped wires or fern pins. Other useful coverings are short pieces of statice, sea heather, yarrow, pearly everlasting, pieces of hydrangea, and so on.

Florist's wire is used to replace the stems, the thickness of the wire depending on the size and weight of the flower head. Before adding the wire stem check the flower to be sure it is free of any particles of the silica gel. Clean it with a soft paint brush if necessary. Hold the flower near the head in one hand and straighten the bent wire, then lay straight along it a wire of correct weight for the flower head.

The wire must then be taped with florist's tape, a stretchy self-adhesive tape. Place the tape at the back of wire, just under the flower head, pressing the sides together; then with one hand twirl the wire gently toward to other hand, which is stretching and pulling the tape downwards till the stem is covered. This task takes a bit of practice, and it is often better to try covering a piece of flowerless wire before starting on the flowers themselves. Don't make the mistake of trying to wrap rather than stretching and pulling the tape.

The upper hand, which is gently twirling the flower and wire, moves down the stem as the stretching of the tape nears the bottom. As each flower's stem is completed, place it in a jar till all are prepared for use; laying them on the table may damage some of the petals.

An outline for the arrangement is drawn with the use of pressed fern, the most-used of all green foliage for this purpose, although dried grasses, twigs, and preserved foliage can be satisfactory, and broom is excellent in achieving a very definite line. A good *green* foliage is the most difficult to get. Snow-on-the-mountain *(Euphorbia marginata)* holds its colour well in silica gel. Eucalyptus treated with glycerine will turn brown, as most leaves do, if left too long in the mixture; try cutting down the amount of time that the material is emersed in the glycerine, in order to retain the natural shade.

A framework made of any one of these materials helps to contain the design. Later on, with a little practice, you may often achieve your desired creation more easily by making the arrangement with flowers alone and completing it with the "fill" later.

Statice is often used as a fill, both to camouflage the mechanical aids and to establish the line of the arrangement.

The fill is more necessary in arrangements of preserved flowers than it is with fresh flowers because it is desirable to hide the artificial stems. Though the arrangements should appear as natural as possible and should be prepared in much the same way as fresh flower arrangements, you probably will have to use more fill. Many arrangers of dried flowers use too much fill, and all of their arrangements look like old fashioned Victorian or Colonial bouquets. The arrangements in this book show that this need not happen.

The fill can be any smaller flower or greenery. Statice, babies' breath *(Gypsophila paniculata)*, pearly everlasting, goldenrod, hydrangea pieces, sea heather, and other materials can be used for this purpose. You must try to use material that fits in well with your choice of flowers. A fill of goldenrods with roses, for example, would be out of place.

All designs used in fresh flower arrangements may also be made with preserved and dried flowers without losing vitality. The sheen and glow and slight movement in air currents which is so exquisite in fresh flowers will not be present, so great care must be taken to have each bouquet so skillfully made that this liveliness will not be missed. By inserting short stems and graduating upward, you can achieve a graceful fall of flower heads, taking away any stiffness from a rigid "heads up" look.

57

Opposite page: A simple and elegant asymmetrical triangle design is created with preserved acidanthera with pieces of grevillea.

A bowl of spring flowers: preserved tulips, narcissus, anemones, hyacinth, freesia, statice, and pressed fern arranged in a convex design.

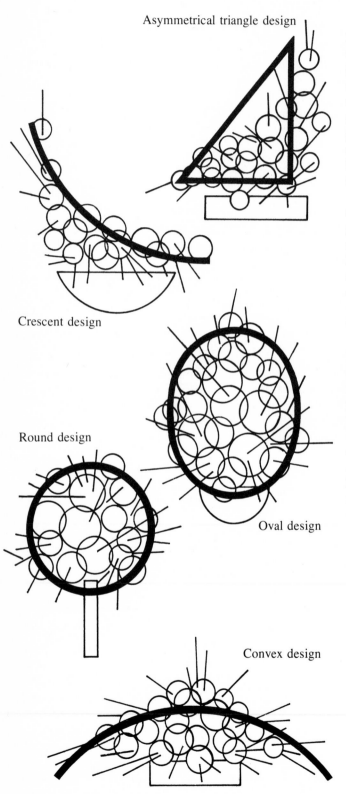

Asymmetrical triangle design

Crescent design

Round design

Oval design

Convex design

The basic **asymmetrial triangle** design developed by the Japanese has symbolic significance. With very few flowers, three basic lines represent heaven (tallest), and earth (shortest), with man in the middle. The lilies you are so proud of will be superb for this, and a few pieces of broom gently curved in the warmth of your hand will hold this curve and give an outline to work within. Daffodils and tulips with pussy willow are also useful for this particular design. The design is an excellent one for beginners, providing a good basic pattern for most arrangements and teaching good proportion, balance, and rhythm.

Strands of broom are good in a **crescent design**, alone or in company with eucalyptus, air-dried or treated in glycerine. Not too many flowers are needed; but those that are available in two or three sizes, as well as buds, several half-opened ones accompanied by one or two full blooms, are quite enough. Keep the large blooms close to the lip of the bowl, and lighten the curve of the crescent as it ascends with the smaller flowers or half-opened buds; then taper off, with a few buds in between.

An **oval design** and a **convex design** are most frequently used for table centrepieces. The oval design is a simple form and provides greater variety and interest. The convex design is well suited to a centrepiece and looks best in a low-pedestaled dish. It can be accomplished easily by using flowers that are not too large, such as roses and ranunculas, interspersed with daintier blooms. Place a few blooms in the centre and fan out in a circular fashion, allowing some blossoms and green to drop below the rim. This particular design lends itself ideally to the mixture of round flowers and spiky flowers. A round design can be more interesting if done in a pedestaled vase.

Black-eyed Susans, sweet clover, vetch, Queen Anne's lace, bunchflowers, and buttercups are gathered in a small oval mass design of preserved wildflowers.

This torch arrangement shows off a perfect lily preserved in silica gel and combined with cattails and moss in a spare, simple arrangement.

The **torch design**, used chiefly with contemporary furnishings, is popular with modern interior designs. The design is exactly what the name implies — a straight up and down arrangement. These arrangements often have a stilted or tortured appearance, and there is a danger that they will look flat rather than three-dimensional. Cut the stems at varying lengths and build from the bottom up, or from the highest point down, whichever way your inclination takes you. A narrow-necked vase with straight lines is the kind usually used in these arrangements.

The famous **Hogarth curve**, or S-curve, boasts of grace and character. As in the crescent, several sizes and shapes of flowers and branches can quickly determine the design. The container for this design must have height to allow for the downward curve.

Torch design   Hogarth curve

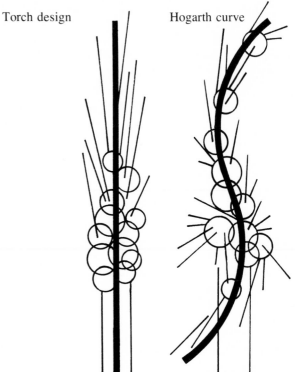

Opposite page: This large mass arrangement includes preserved white rubrum lilies, pink rubrum Martagon lilies, white lilac, peonies, delphinium, and clematis with pressed fern.

Triangular mass design

Preserved black-eyed Susans, scabiosas, honeysuckle, snap-dragons, globe flowers, zinnias and pressed maidenhair fern are combined in an asymmetrical triangle design.

The most pleasing shape for preserved flowers is the loose natural shape perhaps best described as a **triangular mass**, where the paler, more delicate blooms are used on the peri-meter, and the design is closed with the larger flowers and heavier and darker colours near the base, though not always mid-centre. Generally it is more arresting to find this focal point in the arrangement slightly off-centre and set deeper in among the blooms. This shape can be equally successful in a small Victorian vase or a large imposing urn. It is eye-catching on a small side table or strikingly beautiful on a large fine chest.

64

This series of illustrations shows the step-by-step growth of a triangular mass design. Here, the shaped foam is secured in place and hidden under a statice fill, omitting moss.

The fern is added to establish the shape and line.

The arrangement is complete.

These designs we have mentioned can all be made with the simplest flowers, branches, weeds and seed pods. The more natural arrangement, however, is better for preserved flowers than the stiff, formal, linear arrangements. Since the preserved flower arrangements will last many months, the simpler, less stylized arrangement will be easier to live with over a long period of time.

Though you may be swept with enthusiasm and may have a lot of material, do not over-populate your rooms with bouquets. Restrain the urge to place them everywhere. Their charm will surely fade and their unique quality will be lost. Allow those voluptuous peonies and tulips their influence in *one* arrangement. Allow a bowl of ranunculas that you can hardly believe aren't fresh to surprise the eye in one room only. Repetition is jading. Except where there is perfect spot for a startling and dramatic effect, dried flowers should be subtle and should not impose on any of their surroundings. Enjoy their fragility, knowing that you have captured nature for a moment.

Chapter 9 Flowers in Apartments
by Betty Piper

Not everyone is fortunate enough to have a garden. More than 50% of our population lives in our twenty largest cities, and 33% of Canadians live in apartments.

What can you do in an apartment in Montreal, Edmonton or any large city to create a green belt within a cement framework? You can do many of the following things, all of which lead to flower-preserving, the most practical kind of green belt for apartment living.

Become a member of your local botanical garden. Support the parks and playground organizations. Follow the experimental farm and Agricultural Station programmes. Join your local horticultural society. Take courses at the botanical gardens. The botany laboratories at universities throughout the country offer a wide variety of courses in their adult education programmes. VOLUNTEER TO HELP wherever you can on a regular basis, in a shop, nursery, or hospital where care of flowers, plants or gardens is required.

Try to shop at your outdoor market. Hamilton, Kitchener, Toronto, Ottawa, Montreal, and all large cities have fine markets which continue indoors during the winter. You will soon recognize the reliable growers of both vegetables and plants. Buy regularly from them. They will become your good friends.

Seek until you find the florist who is the top expert in dried or preserved flower arrangements. Study this book carefully, and discover how challenging it is to do an arrangement with dried flowers. Take instructional courses whenever they are available. After these first steps, use dried materials that have been dried and stored in your driest, warm cupboard. If possible, have everything ready before spring arrives, because you will be busy.

You *can* grow your own flowers for drying. The average apartment balcony is one of the greatest challenges. Study carefully any information from your local botanical gardens. If you have a southeast or southwest exposure, and you are not exposed to the prevailing winds, treat yourself to two self-watering wooden flower boxes, an awning, and if possible two large deep wooden tubs for your corners beside the building.

Follow the advice of your local botanical garden regarding the flower boxes. Your favourite market gardener will help you by providing the soil mixture prescribed. Grow what is recommended, but check carefully with the index in this book and remember to include lovely ivies, vines and vincas.

For the balcony tubs you might choose roses: two Woburn Abbey plants in front of one Summer Sunshine; and two or three Tropicana, depending on the size of the tub. These would require regular spraying as well as pruning as you

67

cut your blooms. These will provide pleasure, indoors and out, when preserved in silica gel. When the first frost comes, cut the plants down and give them to a friend with a garden.

If spring arrives and you have no flowers, advertise in your area, by newspaper, or at your flower shop or your botany classes: "Will water garden and cut back dead flowers for absentee gardeners in exchange for the privilege of cutting a few fresh flowers". Carry a sack, and in it a deep pot. Pop the flowers into about two inches of water. Rattle on home and have fun with your silica gel, all ready and waiting for you.

If ever anyone suggests a day in the country, pack your bag with care. Cutters, elastic bands, a thermos of water, a deep pot, and your picnic. You will come upon the most lovely weeds and reeds and seed pods by any roadside or along a farmer's fence. Defoliate them and hang as described in this book, on the clothes hook in the car, and later place them in your driest cupboard. Split the stems of the leaves and place in water in the deep pot, adding glycerine when you reach home.

Did you know that your indoor spring bulbs should be stored in your fridge until you have a chance to pot them? Pot them at the proper time in the fall. Line your empty rose tubs (still on the balcony) with straw. Place a row of pots in the tub. Cover them with straw, then put in another layer of potted bulbs. Cover well with more straw and then a plastic bag, well secured. The cold and the snow will come; the pots can be brought into the apartment a few at a time and placed in your coolest cupboard, watered and brought slowly and gradually into the light.

Paperwhites are also lovely. Place the flowers in bowls, support them with white stones and place them directly in the light.

All or any one of these projects can lead to the preservation and drying of plants. In many ways, dried material is much more satisfactory in the average apartment than live plants. Also, in the final analysis, they are much less expensive. The dry atmosphere in apartments, which can be devastating to live flowers, is perfect for preserved ones.

Before long, you will have your own green belt, and it will begin to grow. Your neighbours and friends will take interest too. Perhaps by showing an interest in the planting around your apartment house, you will encourage the owner to make a few improvements.

You can use your own resources to make use of free materials available in cities. For example, a pile of evergreen branches which have been pruned off trees can make sprays and swags from "garbage". Odd "weeds" can be found in vacant lots and along railway tracks.

Perhaps someday your arrangements of preserved flowers will win prizes in a flower show. Until then, good luck!

An asymmetrical triangle design containing preserved daffodils with air-dried grevillea, and pearly everlasting.

Chapter 10 Table of Plant Material for Preserving, Drying and Pressing by Ancilla Deghenghi

The following table is by no means complete or definitive, but it is indicative of the number and kind of flowers, leaves, seedpods, grasses, and ferns which you might be able to collect and dry. For the purposes of the silica-gel method, only the ones which dry true to their original form and colour have been included, with few exceptions. Practically all flowers can be preserved, though some may look in the end a bit less than natural. You might want them anyway, perhaps for sentimental reasons.

So do try experimenting with flower preserving, even if your favourite flowers are not on the list.

The common names of plants vary in different geographical areas, so the botanical names have been included in most cases. Every plant from the time of Linnaeus has been given two names: the first called the genus, and the second, the species. These are accepted and known internationally. In a few cases where the names have not as yet been stabilized, you may find a discrepancy between those in your garden and those used here. In the tables, the suitability of the plant materials for preserving in silica gel is rated as follows:

**** excellent

*** very good

** fair

* questionable

The following botanical guides have been used in preparing the tables in this chapter.

Bailey, Mary — *A Dictionary of Flowers*. (Mayflower Edition, Cox & Wyman Ltd., London, England, 1969.)

Frankton, C. and G. A. Mulligan — *Weeds of Canada*. (Canada Department of Agriculture, Ottawa, 1971.)

Pizzetti, Ippolito and Henry Cocker — *Il Libro dei Fiori*. (Ed. Garzanti, Milano. 1970.)

Schauenberg, Paul — *Les Plantes Bulbeuses*. (Ed. Delachaux & Niestle, Suisse, 1964.)

Time-Life Encyclopedia of Gardening — *Perennials*. (Time-Life Books, New York, 1972.)

Tonzig, S. — *Bontanica*. (Universita Delgi, Studi di Milano, 1956.)

Touring Club Italiano — *La Flora*. (Milano, 1958.)

Wilson, Lois — *Chatelaine's Gardening Book*. (MacLean Hunter Ltd., 1970.)

In addition, the seed and plant catalogues of the following suppliers were consulted.

W. H. Perron Ltd., Montreal

C. A. Cruickshank, Toronto

Sheridan Nurseries, Montreal and Toronto

Silica Gel Method

Name	Harvest Time	Drying Time (Days)	Additional Information
Garden Flowers			
ACACIA**** *Acacia*	Spring	2-3	Bush or small tree; all varieties; pick spray with leaves
ACIDANTHERA **** *Acidanthera bicolor*	Fall	3-4	Corm
ALLIUM **** *Allium giganteum*	Summer	7	Bulb; a bit smelly
AMARYLLIS **** *Amaryllis*	Winter	6-7	Bulb
ANEMONE DE CAEN **** *Anemone coronaria*	Fall	2-3	Rhizome
ASTER **** *Aster alpinus* *Aster Amellus*	 Spring Fall	 2-3 2-4	 Perennial; delicate Annual; delicate
BALLOON FLOWER **** *Platycodon grandiflorus*	Summer	3	Perennial
BELLFLOWER **** *Campanula carpatica* *Campanula cochlearifolia*	 Summer Fall	 3-4 2	 Perennial Perennial
BEE BALM (bergamot, Oswego tea)* *Monarda didyma*	Summer	3-4	Perennial
BELLS OF IRELAND **** *Molucella laevis*	Summer	3-4	Annual; pick spikes or sections
BLUE LACE FLOWER ** *Trachymene caerulea*	Summer	3	Perennial; delicate
BUGLEWEED *** *Ajuga reptans rubra*	Spring	3	Perennial
BUGLOSS **** *Anchusa myosotidoflora*	Summer & Fall	2-3	Perennial
BUTTERFLY BUSH **** *Buddleia Davidi*	Summer & Fall	4½	Bush
CAMELIA **** *Camelia*	Spring	4-6	Bush; all varieties; pick flowers with leaves

Name	Harvest Time	Drying Time (Days)	Additional Information
CANDYTUFT **			
Iberis sempervirens	Spring	3	Perennial
Iberis affinis	Summer	2-3	Annual
CANNA *	Summer	4	Rhizome
Canna indica			
CANTERBURY BELLS			
(cup & saucer) ****	Spring	3-4	Perennial
Campanula calycanthema			
CARNATION ***	Spring &		
Dianthus	Summer	3-4	Perennial; all double varieties
CLEMATIS ****	Summer	3-4	Very delicate
Clematis Jackmannii			
COLUMBINE ****	Spring &		Perennial; all varieties; fill spurs
Aquilegia	Summer	2-3	and trumpets first; very delicate
CORAL BELLS ****	Summer	2-3	Perennial
Heuchera sanguinea			
CORNFLOWER (bachelor's			
button) ***	Summer	3	Annual; delicate; pick when
Centaurea Cyanus			young and fresh
COSMOS ***			
Cosmos bipinnatus	Summer	2	Annual; delicate
Cosmos sulphureus	Summer	2	Annual; delicate
CUPID'S DART ***	Summer	2-3	Annual
Catanache caerulea			
CYCLAMEN ****			
Cyclamen neapolitanum	Fall	3	Tuber
Cyclamen persicum	Fall	4-6	Tuber
DAFFODIL ****	Spring	4-6	Bulb; all trumpet, cup,
Narcissus			and jonquil varieties
DAHLIA ****	Summer &		Tuberous root; all pompon,
Dahlia	Fall	4-5	single, ball varieties
DAY LILY ****	Summer	4-6	Bulb; all varieties
Hemerocallis			

Name	Harvest Time	Drying Time (Days)	Additional Information
DELPHINIUM **** *Delphinium elatum*	Summer	2-3 3-5	Perennial; all varieties Spikes Individual blossom; fill spur first
DEUTZIA **** *Deutzia*	Spring	1-2	Bush; pick sprays
DOG'S TOOTH VIOLET ** *Erythronium Dens-canis*	Spring	3-4	Bulb
DOUBLE BUTTERCUP **** *Ranunculus asiaticus*	Summer	3-4	Tuberous root
*DRYAS ***** *Dryas octopetala*	Spring	2-3	Perennial; very delicate
EDELWEISS **** *Leontopodium alpinum*	Spring	2-3	Perennial
EVENING PRIMROSE **** *Oenothera biennis*	Summer	2 3	Perennial; Florets Heads and clusters
EXACUM **** *Exacum affine*	Summer	2	Perennial houseplant
FLOSS FLOWER *** *Ageratum Houstonianum*	Summer	2-3	Annual
FORGET ME NOT *** *Myosotis alpestris*	Spring	2	Perennial; delicate
FORSYTHIA **** *Forsythia*	Spring	3-4	Bush; all varieties; pick small sprays
FOXGLOVE **** *Digitalis purpurea*	Summer	2-3 4-6	Biennial Florets Spikes
FREESIA **** *Freesia*	Spring	4 5-6	Corm; all varieties Florets Clusters; use hooked wiring (fine wire) down through trumpet blossom to short stem. For a cluster, loop wire between flowers along main stem, twisting at end to hold.

Name	Harvest Time	Drying Time (Days)	Additional Information
FUCHSIA **** *Fuchsia*	Summer	4	Bush; all varieties; Blossom or spikes — fill trumpet first
GAS PLANT ** *Dictamnus albus, roseus*	Summer	4	Perennial; spike
GENTIAN **** *Gentiana*	Summer	3	Perennial; all blue varieties
GERANIUM ** *Pelargonium*	Summer	4-5	Perennial; pick whole head; delicate
GERBERA *** *Gerbera*	Summer	4-5	Perennial; delicate
GEUM * *Geum sibericum*	Spring	2-3	Perennial
GLOBE FLOWER **** *Trollius europaeus*	Spring	3	Perennial
GOLDEN GLOW **** *Rudbeckia*	Summer	3-4	Perennial; pick when very young; delicate
GRAPE HYACINTH ** *Muscari*	Spring	4-5	Bulb; dry upside down; very delicate
HAREBELL **** *Campanula garganica, rotundifolia*	Summer	3-4	Perennial
HEATH ** *Erica carnea*	Spring	3-4	Bush; all varieties
HEATHER ** *Calluna vulgaris*	Summer	3	Bush
HOLLYHOCK **** *Althaea*	Summer	3-4	Annual, perennial, or biennial; all varieties; individual flowers
HONEYSUCKLE **** *Lonicera sempervirens*	Summer	3-4	Bush; see wiring of freesia sprays; dry whole head

Name	Harvest Time	Drying Time (Days)	Additional Information
HYACINTH ****	Spring		Bulb
Hyacinthus		3-4	Florets
		6-7	Spikes; for individual blossom use hooked wire method, fine wire. For spikes or whole stem, use upright position. Blossoms will dry before the stem. Remove from silica gel in four or five days then hang up on a line to completely dry stock. A heavy wire should be inserted up the stem before drying.
HYDRANGEA ****			
Hydrangea arborescens *grandiflora*	Summer	3-4	Bush; pick whole head or sections
Hydrangea hortensis	Summer	3-4	Bush; pick whole head or sections
ICELAND POPPY **	Spring	3-4	Perennial; pick when very young; very delicate
Papaver nudicaule			
JAPANESE ANEMONE ****	Fall	3	Perennial
Anemone hybrida			
LARKSPUR **	Summer	4	Annual; pick spikes
Delphinium Ajacis			
LILAC ****	Spring	4-6	Bush; all varieties; pick spikes
Syringa			
LILY ****	Summer	6-7 or more	Bulb; all varieties; be careful not to flatten flower. Build silica gel gently around flower to preserve natural shape and curve of petals and stamens.
Lilium			
LILY OF THE NILE ****	Summer		Bulbous perennial
Agapanthus africanus		2-3	Florets
		4-6	Head
LILY OF THE VALLEY *	Spring	3	Bulbous perennial; dry upside down
Convallaria majalis			
LUPINE*	Summer	6-7	Perennial; pick spikes
Lupinus			

Name	Harvest Time	Drying Time (Days)	Additional Information
MAGNOLIA *** *Magnolia Kobus*	Spring	4	Bush or tree; loss of colour
MALLOW (Rose of Sharon) *** *Hibiscus palustris, syriacus*	Summer	3-4	Bush or small tree
MARIGOLD **** *Tagetes erecta*	Summer	4-5	Annual; all varieties
MOCK ORANGE **** *Philadelphus Lemoinei erectus*	Summer	4-5	Bush Pick spray with leaves
Philadelphus virginal	Summer	2-3 4-5	Florets Sprays with leaves
MONKSHOOD **** *Aconitum Napellus*	Fall	2-3 4-5	Perennial Florets Spikes; fill trumpet first
MONTBRETIA **** *Montbretia tritonia*	Fall	5	Corm; pick spikes
NARCISSUS **** *Narcissus Tazetta, poeticus*	Spring	5-6	Bulb; all varieties
NASTURTIUM ** *Tropaeolum majus*	Summer	2-3	Annual; pick when very young and fresh
NERINE **** *Nerine*	Summer	4-5	Bulb
ORCHID *** *Cymbidium*		7	Some loss of colour; cut flower purchased year-round
ORIENTAL POPPY *** *Papaver orientale*	Summer	3-5	Perennial; pick when very young and fresh; delicate
PANSIES ** *Viola tricolor, hortensis*	Summer	3-4	Perennial; colour dulls
PASQUE FLOWER **** *Pulsatilla alpina*	Spring	3-4	Perennial
PASSION FLOWER **** *Passiflora caerulea*	Summer	6	Vine

Name	Harvest Time	Drying Time (Days)	Additional Information
PEEGEE HYDRANGEA **** *Hydrangea paniculata*	Summer	3-4	Bush; pick whole head or sections
PEONY **** *Paeonia*	Spring	4-5	Perennial; all varieties
PERENNIAL PEA **** *Lathyrus latifolius*	Summer	3	Perennial
PETUNIA ** *Petunia*	Summer	4	Annual; only the double varieties
PINCUSHION FLOWER **** *Scabiosa caucasica*	Summer	3	Perennial
PINK ** *Dianthus plumarius*	Summer	2-3	Perennial
PLANTAIN LILY *** *Hosta*	Summer Fall	4	Perennial; florets
POT MARIGOLD ** *Calendula officinalis*	Summer	4	Annual; pick when very young; delicate
PRIMROSE **** *Primula veris*	Spring	2-3	Perennial
PRIMULA AURICULA **** *Polyanthus*	Spring	 2 2-3	Perennial Florets Whole heads; delicate
QUEEN ANNE'S LACE **** *Daucus Carota (hortensis)*	Summer	2-3	Perennial
RHODODENDRON **** *Rhododendron*	Spring	4-5	Bush; all varieties including the azaleas
ROSE **** *Rosa*	Summer & Fall	4-6	Perennial All varieties especially Apricot Nectar, Garden Party, Montezuma, New Dawn, Queen Elizabeth, Tropicana, York & Lancaster. Woburn Abbey, Tiffany, Kalahare
SAGE **** *Salvia Horminum*	Summer	3	Annual

Name	Harvest Time	Drying Time (Days)	Additional Information
SAXIFRAGE **** *Saxifraga decipiens*	Spring	2-3	Perennial
SCARLET SAGE *** *Salvia splendens*	Summer	3	Annual
SHASTA DAISY ** *Chrysanthemum maximum*	Summer	4	Perennial; very delicate
SHIRLEY POPPY *** *Papaver Rhoeas*	Spring	3-5	Annual; pick when very young; delicate
SNAPDRAGON *** *Antirrhinum*	Summer	 3 4-6	Annual Florets Spikes; fill trumpet first
SNOW-ON-THE-MOUNTAIN**** *Euphorbia marginata*	Summer	4	Annual
SPEEDWELL ** *Veronica Teucrium,* *reptans, spicata*	Spring Summer	2-3 2-3	Perennial
SPIREA **** *Spiraea Vanhouttei*	Spring	3-4	Bush; pick small sprays
STAR OF BETHLEHEM**** *Ornithogalum umbellatum*	Spring	3-4	Bulb
STOCK **** *Matthiola incana*	Summer	 3 6-7	Biennial Florets Spikes; individual blossoms and tip can be dried separately and built up to natural-looking stock of flowers by wiring and taping individually and then assembling. Place tip stem at top leaving a long stem (wire) along which the flowers can be added at natural intervals by taping.
SWEET PEAS **** *Lathyrus odoratus*	Summer	3-4	Annual; pick florets or spikes
SWEET SULTAN ** *Centaurea moschata*	Summer	3	Annual; pick when young and fresh

Name	Harvest Time	Drying Time (Days)	Additional Information
SWEET WILLIAM ** *Dianthus barbatus*	Summer	4	Perennial
THRIFT ** *Armeria maritima*	Spring	2-3	Perennial
TULIP **** *Tulipa*	Spring	4-5	Bulb; all varieties
VERBENA ** *Verbena hortensis*	Summer	2-3	Annual
VIBURNUM *** *Viburnum Opulum sterile*	Spring	4-5	Bush; pick whole heads or sections
WATER LILY **** *Nymphaea alba*	Summer	4-5	Perennial
WEIGELIA **** *Weigelia floribunda*	Summer	4	Bush; pick sprays
WISHBONE FLOWER **** *Torenia Fournieri*	Summer	2-3	Annual
WISTERIA ** *Wisteria*	Spring	5	Vine
ZINNIA **** *Zinnia elegans*	Summer	3-4	Annual; all varieties except the cactus-flowered ones

Leaves

Name	Harvest Time	Drying Time (Days)	Additional Information
BUGLOSS ** *Anchusa myosotidoflora*	Summer & Fall	4-5	Perennial
DRYAS ** *Dryas octopetala*	Spring & Fall	3-4	Perennial
DUSTY MILLER ** *Centaurea Cineraria*	Summer & Fall	10	Perennial
GLOBE FLOWER ** *Trollius europaeus*	Spring	3	Perennial
LILY OF THE VALLEY ** *Convallaria majalis*	Spring	3-5	Perennial

Name	Harvest Time	Drying Time (Days)	Additional Information
ORNAMENTAL BASIL ** *Ocimum Basilicum*	Summer	3-4	Annual; dark opal
RHODODENDRON ** *Rhododendron*	all seasons	3-5	All varieties including azaleas
ROSE ** *Rosa*	Summer & Fall	4-5	All varieties especially New Dawn

Wildflowers

Name	Harvest Time	Drying Time (Days)	Additional Information
BELLFLOWER **** *Campanula rapunculoides*	Summer	2-3	
BIRD'S-FOOT TREFOIL**** *Lotus corniculatus*	Summer	2-3	
BLACK-EYED SUSAN*** *Rudbeckia hirta*	Summer	3	Perennial
BLOODROOT ** *Sanguinaria canadensis*	Spring	2-3	Protected
BUTTERCUP **** *Ranunculus acris*	Summer	2	
CANADA ANEMONE **** *Anemone canadensis*	Spring	2-3	Protected
DANDELION **** *Taraxacum officinale*	Spring	3	
FIELD BINDWEED **** *Convolvulus arvensis*	Summer	2-3	
FIELD GARLIC ** *Allium vineale*	Summer	3-4	
FLOWERING RUSH *** *Butomus umbellatus*	Summer	4	
HEDGE BINDWEED **** *Convolvulus sepium*	Summer	2-3	
HELLEBORINE **** *Epipactis helleborine*	Summer	5	Protected

Name	Harvest Time	Drying Time (Days)	Additional Information
HEPATICA ** *Hepatica americana*	Spring	2	Protected
LILY **** *Lilium canadense*	Summer	5-6	Protected
ORANGE HAWKWEED **** *Hieracium aurantiacum*	Summer	3	
OX-EYED DAISY *** *Chrysanthemum leucanthemum*	Summer	4	
PASTURE ROSE ** *Rosa carolina*	Summer	3-4	
RABBIT'S-FOOT CLOVER **** *Trifolium arvense*	Summer	2-3	
RED CLOVER **** *Trifolium pratense*	Summer	2-3	
TUFTED VETCH *** *Vicia cracca*	Summer	2	
VIOLET ** *Viola*	Spring & Summer	2	
WILD MUSTARD *** *Sinapis arvensis* *Brassica* sp.	Summer	3	

Air-Drying Method

Garden Flowers

AMARANTH—*Gomphrena globosa*	annual
ARTEMISIA—*Artemisia albula* "Silver King"	perennial
ARTICHOKE—*Cynara Scolymus*	annual
ASTILBE—*Astilbe* (any variety— when blooms open at base)	perennial
BABIES' BREATH—*Gypsophila paniculata*	perennial
BACHELOR'S BUTTON—*Centaurea Cyanus*	annual
BELLS OF IRELAND—*Molucella laevis*	annual
BLAZING STAR—*Liatris spicata*	perennial
BUTTERFLY WEED—*Asclepias tuberosa*	perennial
CHIVES—*Allium Schoenoprasum*	perennial
COCKSCOMB—*Celosia argentea, cristata*	perennial
COMMON YARROW—*Achillea Millefolium*	perennial
DELPHINIUM—*Delphinium elatum*	perennial
FERN-LEAVED YARROW—*Achillea filipendulina*	perennial
GLOBE THISTLE—*Echinops* "Taplow Blue" (before flowers open)	perennial
HANGING AMARANTH—*Amaranthus caudatus*	annual
HEALTH—*Erica arborea*	perennial
HEATHER—*Calluna vulgaris*	perennial
HELIPTERUM—varieties	
Acroclinium "Roseum"	annual
Acroclinium "Album"	annual
Helipterum Sanfordii	annual
Helipterum Rhodanthe	annual
Helipterum Manglesii	annual
HISSOP—*Hissopum officinale*	perennial
HYDRANGEA—*Hydrangea hortensis*	perennial
Hydrangea paniculata	perennial
LARKSPUR — *Delphinium Ajacis*	annual
LAVENDER—*Lavandula spicata*	perennial
LOVE-IN-THE-MIST—*Nigella damascena*	annual
MATRICARIA—*Anthemis nobilis*	perennial
MESEMBRYANTHEMUM CRINIFLORUM	annual
MONKSHOOD—*Aconitum paniculatum*	perennial
OLIVER SEA HOLLY—*Eryngium Oliverianum* (when flowers turn blue)	perennial
PAMPAS GRASS—*Cortaderia Selloana*	annual
PEARLY EVERLASTING—*Anaphalis* (any variety when in bud)	perennial
SAGE, BLUE SALVIA—*Salvia farinacea*	perennial
SCARLET SAGE—*Salvia splendens*	annual
SEA-LAVENDER—*Limonium latifolium* (when flowers fully open)	perennial
SEDUM—*Sedum spectabile*	perennial
SNEEZEWORT—*Achillea Ptarmica*	perennial

STATICE—*Limonium sinuatum*	annual
Limonium Suworowii	annual
STRAWFLOWER—*Helichrysum bracteatum*	annual
TANSY—*Tanacetum vulgare*	perennial
WINGED EVERLASTING—*Ammobium alatum grandiflorum*	annual
XERANTHEMUM—*Xeranthemum*	annual

Leaves

ALBA POPLAR—*Populus alba*
EUCALYPTUS—all varieties
GREVILLEA—*Grevillea*
GROUND PINE—*Lycopodium*
SCOTCH BROOM—*Cytisus scoparius*
SENSITIVE FERN—*Onoclea sensibilis*

Wildflowers

BURDOCK—*Arctium,* all varieties
GOLDENROD—*Solidago,* all varieties
JOE-PYE WEED—*Eupatorium purpureum*
KNOTWEED—*Polygonum lapathifolium*
MILKWORT—*Polygala*
PEARLY EVERLASTING—*Anaphalis margaritacea*
PUSSY TOES—*Antennaria,* all varieties, in bud
PUSSY WILLOW—*Salix discolor*
RABBIT FOOT CLOVER—*Trifolium arvense*
ROUGH FRUITED CINQUEFOIL—*Potentilla recta,* in bud
THISTLE—*Cirsium,* all varieties
VALERIAN—*Valeriana officinalis*
VERVAIN—*Verbena hastata*
YARROW—*Achillea Millefolium*
YELLOW AGERATUM – *Lonas indora*

Grasses

BARLEY—*Hordeum jubatum*
BLUE GRASS—*Bouteloua gracilis*
BROMUS—*Bromus inermis*
BUNNY'S TAIL—*Lagurus ovatus*
BURGRASS—*Chenchrus*
CORN — *Zea mays*
MANNA GRASS — *Glyceria grandis (et canadensis)*
MILLET — *Setaria veridis*
OATS — *Avena*
ORCHARD GRASS — *Dactylis glomerata*
PENNISETUM — *Pennisetum*
SEA-LIME GRASS — *Elymus arenarius*
WHEAT — *Triticum*

81

Air-Drying or Glycerine Methods

Wild Fruits, Pods, Capsules, Berries and Cones

ALDER—*Alnus* (Catkins)
BARBERRY—*Berberis vulgaris*
BITTERSWEET—*Celastrus scandens*
BUTTON BUSH—*Cephalanthus occidentalis*
COWSLIP—*Primula Auricula*
CURLED DOCK—*Rumex crispus*
DELPHINIUM—*Delphinium elatum*
EVENING PRIMROSE—*Oenothera biennis*
FIELD PEPPER GRASS—*Lepidium apetalum*
FLOWERING RUSH—*Butomus umbellatus*
MARTAGON LILY—*Lilium Martagon*
MULLEIN—*Verbascum Thapsus*
MUSTARD—*Brassica*
PEONY—*Paeonia*
POPPY—*Papaver orientalis*
POT MARIGOLD—*Calendula officinalis*
QUEEN ANNE'S LACE—*Daucus Carota*
RABBIT'S-FOOT CLOVER — *Trifolium arvense*
ROSA—*Rosa blanda* (hips)
SELF HEAL—*Prunella vulgaris*
SHIRLEY POPPY—*Papaver Rhoeas*
SUMAC—*Rhus typhina*
VIRGIN'S BOWER—*Clematis virginiana*
WINTER CRESS—*Barbarea vulgaris*

Garden Seedheads, Pods and Berries

BEE BALM—*Monarda didyma*	perennial
BLUE LACE FLOWER—*Trachymene caerulea*	perennial
CHINESE FORGET-ME-NOT—*Cynoglossum*	annual
CHINESE LANTERN—*Physalis Alkekengi*	perennial
COLUMBINE—*Aquilegia*	perennial
COWSLIP—*Primula Auricula*	perennial
CUPID'S DART—*Catananche*	annual
DELPHINIUM—*Delphinium elatum*	perennial
EUONYMUS—*Euonymus*—berry	perennial
GAS-PLANT—*Dictamus*	perennial
GOURDS	annual
HONESTY—*Lunaria*	annual & perennial
IRIS—*Iris*	perennial
LOVE-IN-THE-MIST—*Nigella damascena*	annual
MALLOW—*Malope*	perennial
MILKWEED—*Asclepias tuberosa* (remove silk)	perennial
PEONY—*Paeonia*	perennial
PINKCUSHION—*Scabiosa*	annual & perennial
POPPY—*Papaver orientale*	perennial
Papaver Roeas	perennial
POT-MARIGOLD—*Calendula officinalis*	annual
SHOOFLY PLANT—*Nicandra*	annual
THISTLE—*Silybum*	perennial
TURK-CAP LILLY—*Lilium Martagon*	perennial

Glycerine Method

Leaves and Flowers
ALBA POPLAR—*Populus alba*
BARBERRY—*Berberis*
BAYBERRY—*Myrica*
BEECH—*Fagus grandifolia*
BITTERSWEET—*Celastrus scandens*
BELLS OF IRELAND—*Moluccella laevis*
CANNA—*Canna indica*
DOGWOOD—*Cornus*
ELEAGNUS—*Eleagnus angustifolia*
EUCALYPTUS—*Eucalyptus*
EUONYMUS—*Euonymus*
HOLLY—*Ilex*
IVY—*Hedera*
LARKSPUR—*Delphinium Ajacis*
MOUNTAIN LAUREL—*Kalmia latifolia*
CHERRY (ENGLISH) LAUREL—*Laurus cerasus officinalis*
MAGNOLIA—*Magnolia grandiflora*
PRIVET—*Ligustrum*
PYTTOSPORUM—*Pyttosporum*
ROSE—*Rosa*—leaves with stem
STATICE—*Limonium sinuatum*

Pressing Ferns

BEECH FERN—*Dryopteris Phegopteris*
BRACKEN FERN—*Pteridum aquilinum*
COMMON POLYPODY FERN—*Polypodium vulgare*
LADY FERN—*Athyrium Filix-femina*
MAIDENHAIR FERN—*Adiantum pedatum*
MOUNTAIN BUCKLER FERN—*Dryopteris*
ROYAL FERN—*Osmunda regalis*

Pioneer Plants

Below is a list of plants grown in Canadian gardens before 1860 which were used for drying.

Celosia—*Argentea cristata*
Helichrysum—*Arenarium*
Achillea—*Ptarmica*
Chrysanthemum—*Parthenium*
(feverfew)

Lunaria annua
Humulus lupulus
Hydrangea quencifolia
Hyssopus officinalus
Delphinium Ajacis
Nigella damascena
Amaranthus caudatus
Lepidium virginicum
Amaranthus hybridus hypochondriacus
Artemisia abrotanum
Tanacetum vulgare

Seed Suppliers

The following is a list of recommended seedsmen who carry seeds of flowers suitable for drying:

Geo. Parks—Greenwood, South Carolina

Stokes Seed—St. Catharines, Ontario

W. H. Perron—Chomedy, Laval, Quebec

Carters Seeds—London, England

Geo. B. Roberts—Favershan, Kent, England

C. A. Cruickshank Ltd., Toronto, Ontario

Dominion Seed—Georgetown, Ontario

Silica Gel Suppliers

Civic Garden Centre
777 Lawrence Avenue East,
Don Mills, Ontario.
416-445-1552
Ask for Flora-Cure

Flower and Green Decorations
4922 Sherbrooke St. West,
Westmount 215, Montreal, Quebec
215-418-9388
Ask for Magiflora

C. A. Cruickshank Ltd.
1015 Mount Pleasant Blvd.,
Toronto, Ontario.
416-488-8292
Ask for silica gel or Flower Dri

W. H. Perron
Chomedy,
Laval, Quebec.
Ask for silica gel or Flower Dri

Bibliography

Barrie and Rockliff, Publishers — *The Pulbrook and Gould Book of Flower Arrangement*. (The Cresset Press, London, 1968.)

Berrall, Julia — *A History of Flower Arrangement*. (Viking Press, New York, 1968.)

Brown, Emily — *Bouquets that Last*. (Hearthside Press, New York, 1970.)

Canning, Mary — *Flower Arrangement*. (Arco Mayflower Handybook, Mayflower Books, London, England, 1969.)

Clements, Julia — *The Julia Clements Book of Flower Arrangement*. (C. Arthur Pearson Ltd., London, England, 1964.)

Condon, Geneal — *The Complete Book of Flower Preservation*. (Prentice-Hall, Inc., Englewood Cliffs, New Jersey, 1970.)

Graves, Joan — *The Ilford Colour Book of Flower Decoration*. (Ebury Press in association with George Rainbird, London, England, 1964.)

Hendricks, Katinka — *Flower Arrangement Week by Week*. (Lutterworth Press, London, 1970.)

McDowell, Pamela — *Pressed Flower Pictures*. (Charles Scribner's Sons, New York, 1968.)

Miklos, Josephine — *Wildflowers in Your House*. (Doubleday & Co., Garden City, New York, 1968.)

Nichols, Beverley — *The Art of Flower Arrangement*. (Collins, London, 1967.)

Stevenson, Violet — *Flower Arranging*. (The Grosset All-Colour Guide Series, Grosset & Dunlop, New York, 1970.)

Index

Note: For individual flowers, please also consult the tables in Chapter Ten, pages 69-84, under the appropriate heading.

A

Achillea 25
Acroclinium 19, 46, 47
Adiantum 26
Air-drying 5, 7, 11-12, 17-19, 32, 45-48, 81-83
  garden berries 82
  garden flowers 81
  garden seed pods 82
  garden seedheads 82
  gathering 47
  grasses 81
  leaves 81
  wild berries 82
  wildflowers 81
  wild fruits 82
  wild pods 82
  wiring 47
Amaranth 12
Ammophila 25
Anaphalis 25
Anemone patens 23
Antennaria 25
Arranging 5, 8, 11-15, 51-66
  chicken wire 54
  containers 51-53
  designs 60-66
  fern outline 57
  fill 57
  floral foam 54
  florist's tape 56
  florist's wire 55
  mechanical aids 53
  moss 54
  pinholder 54
Armeria 25
Astragalus 23
Asymmetrical triangle design 60
Athyrium 26

B

Babies' breath 46, 57
Balcony flowers 67
Barley 25, 47
Beardtongue 23
Berries 24-25, 82-83
Biblical flowers 9
Bittersweet 48
Black-eyed Susan 23, 32
Blazing star 23
Blemished flowers 19-20
Bleuets 25
Bloodroot 27
Blueberries 24
Blue-eyed Mary 25
Blue vervain 24
Bog laurel 24
Botanical Gardens 67
Botanical guides 69
Botany departments 27, 67
Bouteloua 25
Branches 5, 19, 48, 66
Brassica 22
Broom 57
Butter-and-eggs 22
Buttercup 22
Butomus 24

C

Calopogon 24
Calypso 24
Campanula 23, 24
Canadian flower-preserving 11-15
Cattails 46, 47
Chicken wire 54
Chinese flowers 11, 15
Cinnamon fern 26
Climate 7, 8
Clover 24
Collinsia 25
Compositae 22
Cones 47-48
Conservation 21
Convex design 60
Cord-grass 25
Cosmos 41
Cotton grass 25
Cranberry 24, 25
Crescent design 60

Cross-wiring 33-34
Cypripedium 24

D

Daffodils 39
Daisies 22, 41
Daucus Carota 23
Delphinium 23, 38, 47
Deutzia 38
Disbudding 19
Dock 46, 47
Dog's-tooth violets 27
Dried flowers 5, 7, 11-12, 15, 45-49, 81-83
Drying agents 15, 29
Dryopteris 26
Dune grass 25

E

Egyptian (ancient) flowers 9
Elizabeth I 11
Elymus 25
Embalmed flowers 15
Epilobium 24
Ericaceae 24
Erigeron 23
Eriophorum 25
Eucalyptus 57
Eupatorium 24
Euphorbia 57
European flower-drying 9-12
European flowers 9-12
Everlasting 5, 7, 12, 17, 25, 43, 81-82

F

Fairy slipper 24
Fleabanes 23
Ferns 5, 26, 27, 49, 57, 65, 84
Ferrari, Giovanni 11
Field guides 27
Fill 57
Fireweed 24
Floral foam 54, 65
Flowering rush 24

Flowers
  garden 7, 11-15, 17-20, 43, 45, 47, 67-68, 70-78, 81, 83
  imported 7-8
  wild 7, 11-15, 20, 21-28, 43, 45-58, 52, 79-83, 82, 83

G

Galliarda 23
Garden books,
  contemporary 17
  early 12
Gilliflowers 11
Glyceria 25
Glycerine method 5, 48, 57, 68, 82, 83
Golden beans 22
Goldenrod 23, 57
Gomphrena 47
Grains 47
Grama grass 25
Grasses 5, 8, 25, 46, 47, 57, 82
Growing for air-drying 19
Growing season 7
Gypsophila 57

H

Hanging method 45-46
Harebell 23, 24
Harvesting 19-20
  for air-drying 19
  for preserving 20
Hawkweeds 22
Heather 24
Hepaticas 27
Herbals 11-12
Herbs 11-12
Hogarth curve 62
Hooking method 34
Hordeum 25
Horizontal position 38
Horizontal wiring 33-34
Houstonia 25
Hyacinth 38
Hydrangea 54, 57